When Harry Met Vicky
—A Fatal Attraction

When Harry Met Vicky
—A Fatal Attraction

Peter Craggs

Library of Congress Control Number:		2010916585
ISBN:	Hardcover	978-1-4568-1129-7
	Softcover	978-1-4568-1128-0
	Ebook	978-1-4568-1130-3

To order additional copies of this book, contact:
Xlibris Corporation
0-800-644-6988
www.xlibrispublishing.co.uk
Orders@Xlibrispublishing.co.uk
300931

CONTENTS

Memoir Title: When Harry Met Vicky—A Fatal Attraction 13

The Geordie Lad 23

A Refugee from the Mainland 27

The New Arrivals to a Foreign Land 38

Their First Encounter 57

Family Life and the 1960s Era 79

The Unwelcome Addition to the Family 101

The Last Trip Back to the UK 109

The Last Move 132

The Night That Changed Our Lives Forever 147

Trial by Media and the Trial in the Supreme Court of Hong Kong......158

Preparing to Leave Hong Kong 190

A New Life in London and the UK 198

The Return Years to Hong Kong 217

Nearing the End 223

This book is lovingly dedicated to my father and mother.

Foreword

Acknowledgements: My special thanks goes to The Standard Hong Kong which allowed me to use their articles and photographs in covering my mother's court case, the South China Morning Post, The Hong Kong Central Library, The Hong Kong High Court (especially the Registry Department), Hong Kong Government Records Office in Kwun Tong, The Hong Kong Police Force Museum, The Hong Kong Police Force Web site

Personal: I am grateful to these people who supported me in those traumatic times and to some who have inspired me to complete this work

Auntie Millie and Uncle Toto's family and son, Paul, and Sister, Kathy, Auntie Rita and Uncle Stan, Auntie Sally and Uncle Hugh, Auntie Lily Sylvia and David, Uncle Charlie and Auntie Mimi, Helen A Lo and Co., Miles Jackson-Lipkin QC, Hong Kong Chief Justice Sir Ivo Rigby. My special thanks to the wonderful author Martin Booth, whose book, *Gweilo*, which I initially avoided reading for a few years because I thought it was just another Englishman's rather patronising account of his privileged lifestyle in Hong Kong. Once I read it in 2008, it inspired me to trace my childhood experiences in Hong Kong and tell the story (well not as pleasant as Martin's) of my relationship to my parents and the life we had there. My sincere condolences go to his family since Martin Booth passed away in 2004.

I decided to write this memoir of my parents because I was finally able to come to terms with the whole event that so drastically changed my life and that of the others in the family. It will have been forty years since my father's death (three years since my mother left me), and for much of those prevailing years, the others and I have struggled through life and have somehow survived the trauma and kept 'our head above water'. Certainly, for me, I was in denial of what happened and wanted to just wipe the memory out of my mind like hitting the delete button, and the whole saga would be gone forever. For much of my adolescent and adult life in London and in the UK, I felt imprisoned by the shame, humiliation, and embarrassment of what had happened to the Craggs's in Hong Kong, and even running away to London could not stop those haunting memories. Needless to say, my way of handling this was to keep a low profile, not share my background with friends or girlfriends, and to function through life with a pretty low self-esteem.

I could have started writing about my experiences while my mother was still alive, but I felt that it was still not the appropriate time to tell the story. I do believe that the catalyst in setting the wheels in motion to start this work was my mother's death at the end of 2008—a final closure of my last parent, who, unfortunately, could never let go of the past and gave me constant reminders when I was around her in the latter part of her life. Being close to her in the last few years, I was able to ask her about her life with my father in the early days, although at times, she would reprimand me if I went too far to know about her personal life—she was still a private person, right up to her final days. I realise that she could only give me her side of the story, and as I was to find out in the research I conducted later, my mother was pretty accurate about all that happened between them. Much of my father's background and his experiences of serving as an inspector in Hong Kong came from my meetings and conversations I had with my father's ex-colleagues in the police force that are still alive today. The impression they gave to me was that my father was a competent and diligent officer and well liked by his fellow peers except for that drinking addiction . . .

It seems that since my mother's death, I was eventually given the sign and the all-clear to embark on the biggest piece of work in my life so far and tell the story. As the saying goes 'a picture can paint a thousand words', certainly the family photographs that I have managed to preserve and include in this book have, I hope, helped to portray what my experiences were like in this Craggs family. I asked my mother again as to why were there so few photographs of the both of them in their happier times together. She said she lost them (or more like she threw them away). What I have displayed in this memoir is all that I have of them, and it's something that I will truly treasure for the rest of my days.

All the material that I have included from my research, the people I met, and the stories and information that I have compiled are solely my responsibility. If there are any mistakes or factual errors in my recollection of events, I would offer my sincere apologies to people and the parties involved.

Memoir Title: When Harry Met Vicky— A Fatal Attraction

Growing Up with My Parents

'Wife cries for joy as she is cleared of murder'

—(Headline: *The Standard, Hong Kong,* 28 March 1972)

'Vicky Victoria Craggs broke down and wept for joy in the Supreme Court yesterday after a jury cleared her of murdering her husband, Police Inspector Charles Henry Craggs.

After deliberating for three hours, the jury of four men and three women decided she was guilty of unlawfully wounding Mr Craggs.

When Mrs Craggs was let out of the prisoner's dock, a woman friend rushed up and embraced her and both wept with joy.

Mrs Craggs was put on $500 bond for two years by the Chief Justice Sir Ivo Rigby.

Sir Ivo said it was neither in the interest of the community nor in that of the children of Mrs Craggs to send her to prison.'

Reported by *The Standard, Hong Kong,* 28 March 1972

From that moment, my life changed forever, and it was a sad and sudden ending of the Hong Kong expatriate experience. As a shy and sensitive twelve-year-old, I wasn't quite sure whether to be happy, relieved, or shocked about all that had happened in the last three months. I knew one thing for sure that all the media attention and the unwanted fame from my parents' case was at long last about to come to an end.

I had had a hard time at school, with some of the kids there teasing me about my parents and making me feel embarrassed and ashamed of my background. It is true that children can be quite cruel, and as much as I tried to keep a low profile, and even with the help of a school friend's family (my best friend) trying to shelter me from all the attention, I really could not escape the unwanted fame or attention in the small Hong Kong. After all, my father was quite well known in the police force (he was known as 'Happy Harry'), and it had come quite as shock to his colleagues and the Royal Hong Kong Police Force that he died so suddenly.

I was puzzled as to why my mother had not contacted us sooner when she was freed, especially as children of hers we were her future and the most important people in her life. When it was reported in the papers that my mother had been released and was free again, she had decided to spend her first day of freedom in a hotel by herself! In fact, I discovered many years later that when she decided to return to Hong Kong in the early 1980s and live on her own, my mother was quite a private person and someone who dealt with her problems by herself.

The first I heard of her release was through a telephone call from Uncle Toto as he enthusiastically said, 'Peter, your mother is free!' When I heard the news, I distinctly felt rather ambivalent about her release and certainly did not feel the joy and relief that I should have felt on hearing such a good news. I knew in my heart that I was happy staying with my 'adopted family', with Paul, Kathy, Auntie Millie, and Uncle Toto. I did not want to return to my family and to all that disaster that had prevailed in the last few months. I wanted to wipe the memory of those people out of my youthful life and almost wanted to create a new identity for myself—I did not want to be Peter Craggs any more! Yet, somehow, I knew that my mother was to be given a second chance at life, and that the authorities would want my mother to head the family and start a new life again with her children. The thought of reuniting with my sister and my half-brother did not exactly inspire me. I had never felt that I had missed something terribly.

The reunion with my mother was a low-key affair, and she had sought help from Auntie Sally for us to meet in a very modest restaurant called the 'Motor Restaurant', which was directly opposite the tram terminus in Happy Valley. I can never forget the day I saw my mother—it was a dark and dingy restaurant, the air conditioning was freezing, and the staff rather grumpy and unmotivated. As I entered the restaurant, Auntie Sally gestured to me to walk to the back of the restaurant, where it was even darker, and the seating was in one of those booth seats where you can almost hide yourself! There she was, my mother, free at last!

When I tentatively approached the table, I could hear her distinctive powerful voice muttering something in Cantonese, and when I came face to face with her, I was shocked at what I saw! She had lost a lot of weight, and she had permed her hair. It was the first time in my life that I had seen my mother do that, and in fact that was the first time in her life she had ever done such a thing to her hair (she always had her hair straight or in the beehive style of the 1960s). I suspect that she had been advised by Auntie Sally and others to change her image, in the light of all the publicity she had received in the media. And yet, when I looked into my mother's eyes for the first time in almost three months, I saw an emptiness and hollowness in her persona, a sort of shell-shocked expression to what she had been through, and a feeling of distance between us. Was this really my mother?

Her first words to me were, 'Are you all right staying with Auntie Millie and Paul?'

'Yes, I like staying with Paul and his family. I feel safe there,' I replied.

My mother's reaction was understandably rather muted and sad, because she realised that she was going to take that safe haven away from me. Auntie Sally interjected and made a comment.

'Your mother is free now, and all of you can start a new life together!' she exclaimed in her optimistic tone.

I did not share my enthusiasm with her! In my heart and mind, I really did not want this. I had got used to the comfort zone of Paul's place and their very Catholic way of living. The thought of starting our life all over again, where we would live, friends, school . . . I was hoping please not . . . . In our brief meeting, with its usual emotions, and my mother still clutching a tissue with her nose, red from sobbing, we did not embrace at all except for me holding her hands for some reassurance. I could sense that even she did not know what our future lives would be, where to turn to, and who could support us in rebuilding our lives. It was surely a daunting prospect that from such a traumatic and difficult trial, my mother, as a single parent with three children, had then been given a second chance to life—to re-emerge from the ashes and ruins of the old Craggs family—to a new identity, and with all the uncertainties of the future that lay before us . . . !

The trial case of my mother had been quite frequently reported in the two main papers—approximately every two weeks in the *South China*

Morning Post and *The Standard*. With all that publicity (unwanted, of course), the students at the school I attended were teasing and taunting me. I remember some of them saying, 'Peter's mother is a killer! Look at that Peter. His mother is a murderer, na, na, na!' And on and on it went. This was all happening at King George V secondary school as it was the local to where we were living in Ho Man Tin. I noticed that some of the friends I had made in school started to avoid me. This is when I knew that I had a big problem and started hated going to school. Even in those days, kids at school could be awful, like today.

The culture in Hong Kong was still predominantly Chinese, of course, especially Cantonese. They had a strong belief in feng shui and were quite superstitious in anything to do with death and trauma. So you can imagine how some of my Chinese friends in the neighbourhood in Ho Man Tin shunned and avoided me on the advice of their parents. I wondered why all those Chinese friends I used to play football and ride bicycle with suddenly had disappeared except for one friend—Paul. I had regularly spent weekends with his family in Happy Valley—encouraged by my father—so that I would not see my parents arguing. To his credit, even in his drunken binges, he still had the concern to protect me from his heated exchanges with my mother.

Paul and his whole family were so sympathetic to what we were going through and knew that I was having a hard time at school. Auntie Millie said now that I would be staying in Hong Kong side, I had to transfer school and the appropriate international school for me to go was Island School. She had hoped that moving me would give me some breathing space from all the teasing and the taunting at King George V, but news travels fast in Hong Kong. I got the same treatment. With my mother under custody and with nowhere else to go, they invited me to stay with them so as to give me some sort of support and a sense of safety. Once that happened, I knew I had a new family to belong to!

Since the night of the stabbing, Paul's strong family bond had made me feel secure and safe in a very traumatic situation. All of us were split up since the incident with my sister, staying with another family and my half-brother, staying with his friends. We did not keep in touch very often, which meant that staying with Paul's family was to offer some sort of comfort for me. Paul's family were strong Catholics and always attended Sunday Mass. The mother, Auntie Millie, even had a huge Virgin Mary statue in her bedroom where we often recited the rosary as a family. From seeing the solidarity and a sense of protection in this Catholic practice, I was really keen to join the Catholic religion since my own parents didn't have any religious convictions. My father, though, was from the Church of England and always kept a Bible, until one day, our dog, Lassie, chewed up the pages, which Dad was furious about! Every time I attended Mass with Paul and saw them taking communion and going to confession, I wanted to participate in this practice to cope with what was going on in my dysfunctional family. I will always be grateful to all of Paul's family for their loving and compassionate support.

On Auntie Millie's suggestion, I was going to be able to visit my mother—an encounter that I felt was both apprehensive and reassuring. Besides who else was going to take me? Auntie Millie was such a compassionate and kind person—she really felt for me and for the rest of my family for such a tragedy to have happened to me especially. She realised how important it was for me to have some emotional bonding with my mother and that a visit to her in prison would still maintain the relationship of mother and son. Auntie Millie contacted Uncle Stan and Auntie Rita, who invited my sister to stay with their family, and she arranged for us to all go together to the prison. Auntie Rita had been looking after my sister, but I found out that she would not be coming to prison. Our half-brother was unavailable, and somehow I knew he didn't really care about visiting our mother. He was such a loner and alienated from the rest of the family—more about him later!

Being naturally shy and sensitive, even more so after what happened, I was really nervous and scared but also keen and curious to see how my mother was doing. Tai Lam Chung Prison is located in Tuen Mun New Territories, a maximum-security prison for women, established in 1969. It incarcerated the most dangerous and serious women offenders in the territory and had a notorious reputation amongst the local population. In those days, Tuen Mun in the New Territories was an undeveloped and remote area—unlike now. It's now a bustling new town with a huge shopping complex, a beach called the Gold Coast, and a twenty-minute drive to Hong Kong International Airport (consistently voted in as the top two airports in the world, and how different from that old Kai Tak Airport!)

Driving to a remote part of the New Territories, where I had never been or even had friends, was a daunting prospect. And, of course, seeing my mother in prison and beginning to realise that my mother may never be free again or to be with us, well . . .

As we were waiting in the visitor's room for my mother to see us, I looked around the place as an inquisitive twelve-year-old would and noticed how everything was so grey—the walls, the tables, the chairs, big metal doors, and the barbed wire that surrounded the outside of the building.

I noticed that women were in uniform, which surprised me because I had only been used to seeing men and, of course, my father in the police uniform. I held Auntie Millie's hand tight; I knew this was not a friendly place! We had a large window to look out to see people coming towards us. I was getting more and more nervous as we were waiting for my mother to see us, and then suddenly in the distance, I saw a short Chinese lady in a white uniform as if she was in a hospital. It was my mother, and she looked like she had been crying a lot. She was being led by a woman in uniform (prison officer), and she looked awful. The door opened, and there I saw my poor mother crying her eyes out as she managed to sit down. She saw me but immediately she hugged and sobbed into Auntie Rita's arms as if she was her own sister! I had never seen my mother so upset and in such a primitive state as if she was like an *armah* (the Chinese servants we had). Her hair was all plain and uncombed, and she had lost a lot of weight. I even noticed that my mother had a big sore on her nose, probably from all that crying and sobbing from all the emotion. My mother realised that I might be scared of her—she was right! My mother was not a pretty sight, especially because I was so used to seeing her wearing fashionable clothes and her hair in the beehive style of the 1960s and early 1970s. I was to find out years later that Auntie Rita and my mother were close friends before they each married their British Expat police officer husbands. They used to share rooms together and worked in the same bars in Hong Kong.

Auntie Rita also broke down, but I felt that her emotions and tears were not sincere and that she had put on a show to demonstrate how much she cared for my mother. My mother really did not like her one bit, mainly because, I think, my mother was jealous of her as she had married a more steady man and that her husband, Stan, was of a higher rank than my father.

Years later, my mother did share with me that they were very close when they used to cruise the bars in Kowloon and Wan Chai and had almost become like sisters until a big fallout over something. That something was never revealed to me, but knowing my mother, and the business they were in, all the bitchiness and jealousy eventually broke up their friendship. Still, Auntie Rita did take in my sister and let her stay with her children, and of all the Chinese wives of British police officers, only Auntie Rita was willing to help us in those difficult circumstances. I am grateful to her and Uncle Stan.

My mother was clearly suffering in prison and because of seeing her so distressed, and she realising it might scare me away, I sat at a distance, with Auntie Millie holding me tight to reassure me. I did eventually hug my mum, but I think she was so absorbed in her own emotions that there was not much talk between us. We left after about an hour, with my mother being led back to her cell. One of the saddest days of my life!

With the case continuing at the Supreme Court and the media giving regular updates, I had settled in quite well into Paul's family. I remember how caring they were when Kathy, Paul's elder sister, deliberately hid some the news stories of the case from me so I wouldn't see all the distressing details.

At least a month had passed since our last visit, and Auntie Millie asked if I wanted to visit my mother again. I was missing her, and the delayed reaction of the shock on seeing my mother in such a state made me keen on seeing her again. This time, though, we went by ourselves to Tai Lam Chung—and what a difference there was in my mother's condition! When I saw her this time, there were none of the raw emotions and sobbing, and now she looked more settled and accepting of her situation. She had put on weight, her hair was combed, she looked smarter, and, most of all, she acknowledged that she had committed a serious crime. They say, in counselling and personal development, once you accept your situation, a sort of peace and tranquillity comes over you. Again, I was to find out later from my mother that she had almost given up on life and had resigned to spend the rest of her life in prison. She even told me that she had made some friends with other inmates that had triad (organised crime gangs) connections, and that one of them promised my mother to get her released on the condition she would join the gang after her release. If my mother would join them, they promised her that her children—all of us—would not have to worry about food and shelter. Considering my mother's predicament and with an uncertain future for all us, I suppose you could say it wasn't a bad offer! How dramatic life could have been, or a twist of fate, if my mother had accepted the offer!

The Geordie Lad

My father was born in 1928 into a traditional north-east town, South Shields, England, now a suburb of the city Newcastle upon Tyne. The timing of his birth could not have been harsher or more difficult as his early childhood was right bang smack in the middle of the Great Depression of the early 1930s that followed the 'Wall Street Crash' of 1929 in the US. South Shields, formed part of the larger area known as Tyne and Wear and was known for its shipbuilding yards of Jarrow and Tyneside and the mining collieries of Chichester, North Shields, and Gateshead. It's affectionately known as 'the land of the Geordies'! Both my father's parents were typical working class, and my father's mother 'Nana' was Scottish. He was the younger of the two siblings with an elder sister, Mable. My father had a close but temperamental relationship with Nana, which I saw as a young six year old when we stayed at Nana's place in Spohr Terrace, South Shields in the mid-1960s. My father excelled at football at school in South Shields and played in the school team as the goalkeeper—something I too did well at school in Hong Kong and then in London later. He did his national service since leaving school and even served in Palestine during the creation of the Israeli State in 1948 (his specialty, I am told, was that he drove army trucks). After doing his term, he returned to the UK, which, at that time, was pretty depressing, especially after the end of the WWII. There were limited job prospects in Tyneside in those days—either the shipyards of Tyne and Wear or the pit mines—neither of which had appealed to my father.

Fortunately for him, his father advised him not to go down the mines, mainly because the danger of the mines, especially in those days and also the unhealthy work conditions. The shipyards were also risky and a dangerous job because of frequent accidents in the massive steel and iron works. It was also a very 'closed-shop' work environment as people got in either through generations of working there, or those that got jobs there knew someone who knew someone. His only other option was to join the North Shields Police Force in 1949-50. Considering his build and stature, six foot two, he was ideally suited to join the force. It seemed a good career move, and as he settled in well in the force, serving his local community, he became popular with his neighbourhood and close to people that he cared for and liked—the one important one being the relationship he had with his cousin, Audrey—more about her later). Again, he excelled at football in the force and became the first-choice goalkeeper in the Northern Police Force and actually won the 1949-50 Northern Police Challenge Cup—this he also carried on to the Hong Kong Police Force and won medals there as well. So with that achievement and being popular, or dare I say it, a hero amongst his colleagues, life as a bobby on the beat in North and South Shields was pretty good considering the hard times of post-war Britain. I was to find out when I visited South Shields and Newcastle a number of times, life was centred around the drinking culture of the pubs, and even more so in my father's time of post-war and 1950s Britain. Besides, what else was there to do in that cold north-east wind of Geordie land! Understanding my father's upbringing and the culture of his time, going to the pub and drinking started at a very young age in those days—probably fourteen to fifteen years for him. That's where you met your friends, colleagues, work discussion, relaxing (chilling out literally), getting away from the family and the wife! My mother even told me years later that Grandmother Nana, who herself was a regular drinker (no surprise there!) used to add some brandy or whiskey to my father's milk bottle to make him sleep, before she went on her night out. I remember quite vividly on our one and last stay in South Shields with Nana, in the mid-1960s, that before we went to bed (usually 9.00 p.m.), she would always give us a mint sweet, and then off she would go to the pub, painting lipstick, and dressed up ready for the local. So with that history and that overwhelming peer pressure of pub culture, I knew my father had a drink problem!

His relationship with Cousin Audrey was close—unusually close. Looking back at some of the pictures of my father on South Shields beach (actually quite a nice sandy one, when it's warm enough!) and with Audrey by his side having a good time, there was something not quite right about the two of them. He was clearly fond of her, and she was delighted to be with him. Every time my father mentioned Audrey when we were visiting South Shields, my mother would get annoyed and suspect something more was going on. Years later, I was to find out that my mother told me of their incestuous affair that had started in their teens and that Grandmother Nana was their matchmaker! No wonder my father had a fraught relationship with Nana. I think my father felt very guilty about the relationship, which probably drove him to drink more. To add more stress to my father, Audrey became pregnant and gave birth to a daughter in around 1950-51, which would mean that I have a half-sister into her sixties up to the present day. I would imagine in those days contraception was not very advanced (the pill was introduced in the early 1960s) and certainly there was no DNA testing. I made a visit to see Audrey—I had never met her before, but thanks to my mother who encouraged me to know more about this Audrey—and drove up to North Shields in late 1990s, having been able to track her down.

When I met her then, she was a frail woman in her early sixties, working part-time in as cashier in a local Safeway supermarket. My main reason to visit her was to ask her whether it was true that she did indeed have an incestuous relationship with my father. She flatly denied all of it and actually became quite upset that I would ask a question about this. I never saw her again after that, and to this day, I don't know whether it was true or not. However, Audrey did confirm to me that she had a daughter whom I have never met before and that she lives somewhere in the northwest of England. I did see one picture of her, and she had an uncanny resemblance to my father!

So, to my father, this event that had taken place well before my mother or any of us had arrived on the scene had quite clearly upset him in his life then. It affected his work and future in the North Shields Police and his future in the UK. He knew it was wrong and that the alleged fact that he bore a child with Audrey, played havoc with his conscience and his principles. With all this happening and probably getting too much for him, an escape route was offered to him to leave this mess behind . . . a far away exotic culture and a land of the British Empire, and all the trappings of an exciting privileged expatriate life—joining the Hong Kong Police Force! For a young twenty-three-year-old Geordie lad, I can understand why he made the decision to accept an offer of a lifetime and make the journey to the crown colony of Hong Kong—a tropical land that offered sun, sea, sand, and sex—it sounds a bit more glamorous than South Shields!

A Refugee from the Mainland

At least my mother and father had one background they shared from the outset—poor traditional working-class families. Except that, my mother's family were more desperate as poor farmers and struggling to make a daily living. Born in a Chinese village of Xiaogan, near the town of Hankow Hubei Province, sometime in the early 1920s (it's an estimate of her birthday because China did not keep birth records in those days). She was the firstborn to her father Wu Bong Ming. My mother told me that being a first child and a girl was a great disappointment to her parents—Chinese tradition always believes that having a son was auspicious and fortunate for the family and status. Also, she was told that she was born feet first, which was seen as an unlucky sign for the family, according to all sorts of strange superstitions that dominated village life in those days, so not a great start for her life. They were at times, as my mother recalled, desperately poor, with her father struggling to feed the family. Growing up in Xiaogan, Hubei, a central province of China, did not help either as it had none of the advantages of being near the sea or a major river running through it to provide the town's population with natural food resources. Of course, times have changed now with the capital city Wuhan having been established as a major industrial centre of China with the great Yangtze River flowing through it. The time of the 1920s in Nationalist China was still a poor

27

corrupt feudal system, with the lingering influence of the last Qing Dynasty Empress Dowager Cixi, and the country had tremendous problems in the increasing divide between the rich and the poor—mostly landowners. With the influence of Lenin and Trotsky and the Russian Bolshevik Revolution, China was next on the list of Communist Revolution—to be led by, then a poor, little known revolutionary student called Mao Zedong!

So, her father worked like most of the poor Chinese masses as a farmer. He grew local crops near their small farmland next to the mud-hut home of theirs and carted the produce to the local market to sell. My mother still cries when she tells of the heartache she felt for her father working so hard on the land to keep feeding the family, and like a donkey or mule, carted the vegetables to the market. Realising that times were hard and could just about fend for themselves, they decided to give my mother away when she was around two or three years old to the second wife, whom she called her stepmother.

Polygamy was the norm in those days, especially in the countryside. My mother never really recovered from that trauma, and it haunted her for the rest of her life. She really hated her stepmother, who, she claimed, just treated her like a domestic slave at the home with little or no emotional bond. Her parents were to try again for more children (certainly no one-child policy then!), especially boys, and they certainly got a bucket full! They, in fact, produced three or four sons and a further three daughters over the years—no fertility treatment required there! My mother estimated that she was one of seven children, and she took some comfort in that she was not alone. However, tragedy struck—all were to die except for one stepsister, in near infancy, due to measles, chickenpox, diarrhoea, and cholera. It was the sign of poverty in that era of China and not having access to vaccines, in order to treat infants with immunisation from such diseases. According to my mother, her parents were such strong believers in traditional Taoism that they believed that gods would somehow answer their prayers, and they would somehow gain help and divine intervention to save their lives and those of their children. How wrong they were! My mother was alone again, with a stepmother that she loathed. My mother was desperate for a way to escape . . . !

A natural talent that my mother was born with was singing (something I enjoyed and did well at school as well) and she loved the Chinese Peking Opera—an art that was flourishing in pre-Communist revolution! This not only gave her pleasure, but also a valuable opportunity of getting out of the house and away from that stepmother of hers. She joined the local Opera group in Hankow Town Centre, and there she was able to make friends and some useful work contacts. By this time, when she was in her late teens, the Japanese had already invaded China in 1937-38. She had a junior role as a singer in the opera troupe. This troupe was planning to travel to various regions of China, such as Changsha Hunan, Chengdu Sichuan, Shanghai, and Kunming and perform at local theatres. All this was happening at the same time as the Japanese were conquering the north and moving south very rapidly. My mother jumped at the chance to travel with the troupe, especially to avoid the sense of imprisonment from the stepmother. Although she was desperate to get away, she was still close to her real mother and father and was very upset to leave them behind. The war was intensifying, with the Japanese raping, pillaging towns, cities, and reports of horrifying stories of mass murder and torture (Rape of Nanjing 1937-38) were coming. It was then that her parents encouraged her to escape further south and west so as to escape the Japanese, who had a voracious appetite in raping and killing young Chinese women. Therefore, it was a matter of life or death for her to join the troupe and outrun the Imperial Japanese Army. Elderly people were relatively safe from the Japanese. There were some true horror stories that my mother shared with me. When Japanese soldiers captured Chinese men, either soldiers or civilians, it did not matter which, then keeping them prisoner and almost starving them was too boring. So, to entertain themselves as well as to get rid of so many POWS, they amused themselves and practised their fighting skills by putting individual men in rice sacks for them to do bayoneting practice. For women, it was even more horrifying—after raping them, they tied them to trees and would round up wild dogs, whip them up to a mating frenzy, and get the dogs to impregnate the women! One could only shudder at the thought of what other torturous practices the Japanese did to the Chinese population, who they once labelled as 'no better than ants!'

On her personal escape from death, she told me how she had survived a Japanese zero plane that dived, bombed, and rattled its machine gun bullets on their open-top train that was meant to be used for transporting cattle. People were crowded on to the train, which was the only form of mass transport there, desperately trying to escape the Japanese zeroes that were swarming over the area, spraying their hundreds of rounds of bullets. My mother described it as a massacre as if the Japanese pilots were doing some shooting practice. People fell around her like sacks of potatoes, and blood was spraying everywhere. She was covered in blood and thought that she was hit and would die—when, in fact, it was all the other people's blood that splashed on to her! Truly horrifying and my mother never forgave the Japanese right up until her death!

So all through the war, from 1937-45, longer than in Europe—1939-45, my mother was running to save her life. The abrupt ending of the Japanese occupation and the war occurred when the US deployed their B-52 bomber planes and dropped two atomic bombs on the cities of Hiroshima and Nagasaki in 1945—an event my mother recalls was such a relief for her and the rest of the Chinese nation who had suffered horrendously under Japanese occupation. Around that time, my mother said she was travelling with the troupe in Southwest China and became friendly with a fellow male colleague and entered into a relationship. Out of their affair, she got pregnant and produced a daughter. See Yee was born in 1942—something she bitterly regretted—to have a child with this man! It was the height of the war as the Japanese were bearing down in central China.

Realising that she had to keep running, she decided to leave the daughter behind to be cared for by the father and the in-laws. And added to the fact that to give birth and not be officially married was frowned upon in those days, so my mother was potentially facing embarrassment and ridicule on her return home after the war. On the one hand, the war had ended, with the young Mao hailed as the hero in fighting the enemy, but the price paid by the Chinese people was the initial creation of the Communist Movement led by Mao—the People's Republic of China. You would've thought that war was over, and the country could heal and rebuild itself after such turmoil—but no, another war had to be won against (indeed started pre-war) the Nationalists led by Chiang Kai-shek. Mao claimed that the Nationalists were traitors to the Chinese people because he claimed that Chiang would sell out to the Japanese and try to have a part in taking over China if the Japanese had won the war.

My mother was never a fan of Mao and Communism, and I can understand why. Since in her youth, she liked the glamour of Opera, western colonial influence in Shanghai, and all that music and Western lifestyle—a sense of freedom she felt! She mentioned to me that her favourite on-screen idols were Gregory Peck and Tyrone Power (which I still have the pictures of) and these movies were shown in local theatres. It was also my mother's first opportunity to hear and learn English, albeit American English. She also shared with me a tender story of when she was in Chongqing Sichuan and met some U.S. airmen based there. It was her first encounter with a European (blond-haired and blue-eyed, no doubt), and she recalled how friendly they were and offered her chocolates and bubble and chewing gums! She was totally fascinated by the gum—and to be able to blow bubbles in your mouth was out of this world and unheard of in China! From that experience, my mother formed a rather naïve impression that Westerners (especially American men) were much kinder, more fun loving, and gentlemanly than her own native men!

Significantly, her stay in Shanghai was to influence for the rest of her life! She always reminisced about the elegance of the old decadent ways of tea dances, relishing in putting on Cheong Sam (elegant Chinese dress) and watching Hollywood movies of the 1940s. She raved about the place, and if it wasn't because of the Communists revolution (which actually started in Shanghai Renmin (People's) Square, taking over the city, she said she would've stayed. Shanghai was the most important Chinese port in East and already had significant European presence there, and from that, it developed into a metropolis of entertainment, culture, and wealth. It was seen as perfect fusion of the East and West, and everyone wanted to be there—including my mother!

From around 1946-48, she had made quite a lot of friends and became very fluent in Shanghainese, and I recall quite vividly that most of my mother's old friends were from that city. Not afraid of the limelight and some kind of a natural performer, my mother had learnt how to dance the waltz, foxtrot, jive, and tango to quite a professional level in the clubs and bars of Shanghai. She had mingled for the first time more intimately with Westerners who were still based there. Shanghai was a sophisticated seaport, with a substantial amount of European presence, and a flourishing shipping and manufacturing base. It was the place to be in—pre-Communist China!

The famous Shanghai Bund has an array of Western architectural buildings (not much change today) which earlier had been built for European embassies and consulates, and has a striking resemblance to the Albert Embankment in London, but only bigger! How my mother hated the Communists for destroying all that was artistic, of culture, class, and sophistication.

With such excitement and experiencing the lavishes from a Chinese city, not that far away from my mother's hometown, she must've thought this was a gift from heaven! My mother was in her mid-twenties by then, and fortunately, for her, she was blessed with the classic glass-shaped figure and a healthy bust to go with it! I suppose it was the natural path to follow in those days, and as the saying goes 'if you got it, then flaunt it'! With these natural assets and her extroverted persona, she was snapped up by a scout for a manager of the nightclubs around the Bund area and started working as a dancing/bargirl. There was a high demand for these women to provide entertainment for the European and American armed forces passing through the port, but they also served the local affluent businessmen who were notorious in keeping mistresses in their leisure time. I was always amazed how knowledgeable my mother was in naming so many movie stars of the forties from Bette Davis, Joan Crawford, Joan Fontaine, to her idolising Gregory Peck, Tyrone Power, and Montgomery Clift. From watching these movies, and how influencing they were to the audience in those days, my mother did think, 'These Westerners (*gweilos*) really do have it good, and I want a piece of it myself!' It was from that media that my mother picked up Pidgin English, something of a great achievement for her, coming from where she came from. I was also amazed to discover that she was very proficient in playing card games like poker, black jack, thirteen-card poker, and numerous forms of patience. I had always wondered why my mother had painful feet, and she always complained that she could not stand or walk for long periods of time. I was to discover years later that her feet were bound for a time, a traditional sign of beauty is for women to have small delicate feet, and the expression of excruciating pain gripped her face whenever she wore heeled shoes. To compound the problem for her, the shoes that were in fashion in the business she was working in demanded that women wore four to five inch heeled stilettos, with the intention of greater sex appeal to the clients she was serving. My mother was not tall but average, from where she came from, standing at five feet one inch, and adding another four to five inches to her height from those stiletto shoes made a big difference in terms of her appearance and sex appeal—after all, she was in competition with other female colleagues! We know now how damaging these shoes are to the feet, and the sight of my mother's bunions at an almost forty-five-degree angle to her front toe, the disfigurement, and the pain caused, plagued my mother for the rest of her life. She still insisted it was a price worth paying for (more stories later) in entering this type of work, because the alternative was hell, she recalled.

Her first working experience was in a factory near her village, which she described as the most distressing and miserable chapter in her life—it was literally working in a fortified factory, locked into the grounds, and workers would sleep and eat there upon finishing their fourteen to sixteen hours shift. She swore to herself that she would rather end her life than tolerate such an existence. But underneath the glamour and the ostentatious lifestyle of the Shanghai night scene, there was still the hard graft of making money by entertaining this clientele, and although my mother insisted it was strictly dancing and chaperoning activities, there were still the 'icing on the cake' service available—sex. Considering my mother's attractiveness and a certain 'joie de vivre' attitude to life then, she did offer the service (probably under certain duress from her manager) to her clients at additional cost on top of the dancing and entertaining package of services. And why not— this was Shanghai, the Paris of the East—a Mecca of nightlife for the European shipping and business contingent, which offered something quite unique in the world then—a cosmopolitan city, which seemed to capture the perfect fusion of an eastern and Western culture. As my mother said, if you had the money and connections in the city, nearly every form of entertainment, lavish lifestyle, and personal services would be served by the most elegant, attractive, and vivacious of women in China. It was the envy of the world!

Alas for my mother, this brief window of Shanghai paradise for her was to end with Mao's Red Guards gaining the masses' support to overthrow the old China. It's no wonder that the movement started in Shanghai as it was the model of a drunken class based system that excluded the majority of the peasant population. Everything my mother treasured, the fashion, the elegant dresses, the etiquette, the music, anything literary, was burnt and destroyed with the slogan of 'foreign pornographic and drugged-up Western ways, possessing the people.' My mother was so passionate about Peking opera, and when that was officially banned by the Communist Party, it broke her heart. The China she knew had metamorphosed into a horrible Communist machine monster, with its people being enslaved and blindly following the god-like leader Mao. My mother commented that 'everything became ugly in China, its people, the land, the hearts of the people, and that terrible Mao uniform.' It was time for her to run again (like so many others) and find a future . . .

Once the war was over and my mother had tasted freedom and a certain amount of Western lifestyle in Shanghai, she turned into a liberated woman, unheard of in China in those days! Still haunting her though was the fact that she still had a daughter whom she had abandoned back in her hometown in Hankow. She decided to go back and see if she could compensate for the lost time of having spent the last six to seven years of See Yee's childhood away from her and probably marry her father properly so as a way to 'save face' (credibility) and try and live as a proper family. However, during the time, she was absent she was already a condemned woman—an outcast—accused of being a heartless mother that did not deserve any better. The marriage was a disaster, lasting less than two years, with my mother alleging See Yee's father as being a drunkard and an abusive man, having ex-marital affairs. Added to this, on her return to her village in Xiaogan, she discovered that her beloved father, Wu Bongming had passed away—a great blow to her support system and the only person she sought comfort in. So with all this happening and feeling totally isolated and indeed ridiculed and condemned, my mother knew she had no future there and made the painful decision to leave that part of her life again forever. Only this time, she had grown up and had the Shanghai experience behind, so she felt that that was her moment to lead the life she wanted. The war had ended, but the Communists were coming, which was another tyranny to be avoided. She had tasted freedom like an addict to opium and heard that a tiny British colony, south of Guangzhou, would offer her salvation and freedom—Hong Kong. She had made the decision to leave the mainland forever in search of freedom, love, and security, never to return. As fate would have it, leaving all those people behind, especially her daughter, See Yee, my mother would still have to meet them again some thirty years later and be reunited with them one more time . . . !

The New Arrivals to a Foreign Land

It was an auspicious time in 1952. The Korean War was raging on. Mao's communist revolution had established itself in China to be called the People's Republic of China with the subsequent retaliation of the West (namely the United States) to initiate McCarthyism. This right-wing movement was designed to counter the powers of communist socialist ideals that were a threat to its supremacy—namely, capitalism, democracy, and freedom. Anything that was red was seen as those 'red devils' and evil to the Western society then. After a major world war that ended in 1945, the world had moved into a new era of the 'Cold War', with the East against the West.

By the time my father had arrived in Hong Kong in 1952, the colony was still recovering from the ravages of Japanese occupation. Hence, the reconstruction of its public services, and especially establishing law and order were seen as paramount policy to administer by the Colonial Government. It was also a time of a mass exodus and influx of Chinese from the mainland to escape communist rule, since the People's Republic of China was declared established by Mao in Tiananmen Square on 1 October 1949. It must have been a daunting prospect for my father to venture seven thousand miles east and look for a better future—it's a long way from South Shields, South Tyneside! Travelling there in the early 1950s was conducted by sea, but my mother told me that my father was flown over there by the British government. It was preferred by HM Overseas Civil Service to send junior officers to the crown colony, with the main reason, I guess, to give the young men a taste of international flying (a good morale booster, I suppose) but also to usher them in as soon as possible and get on with the job! As glamorous as it was in those days to fly, it must have been quite a challenge to handle the experience (British Overseas Aviation Corporation or British Caledonian). Commercial jet engines were not yet introduced to the consumer market, and I am sure it must've taken at least a day to travel all the way to Hong Kong (can you imagine the jet lag!) Luckily, for my father, he didn't have a problem with flying, and he told me that it was his first ever time in a plane. He must have felt that this journey was sort of surreal experience—'it is really happening to me and like arriving on another planet?' At the tender age of twenty-three or twenty-four, a Geordie lad from North East England with a very heavy accent (something I could never quite comprehend) landed at Hong Kong's Kai Tak International Airport in 1952. I can imagine the excitement and trepidation he must've felt in arriving to a foreign land and foreign culture, miles away from home and Europe, to be greeted by the recruitment officer of the Hong Kong Police. I don't think my father even ventured beyond the shores of South Shields and UK except for the war in Palestine in 1948, let alone Hong Kong China! At least he was not alone—a band of junior inspectors hired from the UK to enforce the Her Majesty's law in a foreign colonial land. And what a position to start with—Junior Inspector level, which, for my father, was quite an achievement since he had only served two to three years in the South Shields force. Yes, in those days of being a gweilo (a white man) and serving in Her Majesty's overseas civil servant as a police officer were entitled to some great benefits and privileges (more about that later) which my father could only dream of back home. I remember my father telling me that the first that struck him at arriving in Hong Kong was the tremendous heat and humidity that struck him like walking into an oven. As a young and rather brash character from the north-east, his eyes must have been almost 'popping out', seeing the yellow-skinned and short Chinese locals with slanted eyes, darting around going about their business! The Cantonese dialect of the locals must've sounded like a language from another planet to him! (I must admit that when I had my first trip to Mainland China in the early 1980s, I felt the same way too!) So, for all the excitement and the prospects of a bright future, the issues he left behind in the UK still haunted him and for a proud man that he was, it still hurt him and undermined his confidence and self-esteem for the rest of his life, even in faraway Hong Kong.

'You'll make it up, Craggs, if you behave!' (meaning that he had a promising future). These were the words that my father heard from his district commander in the Hong Kong Police Force during his induction and personal interview—something, which each junior inspector had to go through in the first year. Encouraging words indeed, and the senior officers there were looking for a new generation of leaders to continue colonial rule, and my father seemed to be one of those that impressed them. When he first joined the police force as a sub-inspector in 1952, Hong Kong was in a mess in terms of the administration and the establishment of law and order, and it was still licking its wounds from the cruel Japanese occupation that had left some traumatic memories for the local Chinese. Further, consolidation was needed to rebuild Hong Kong, and my father's generation of young expatriates were keen and enthusiastic to learn and extend their comfort zones. Apparently, the orientation programme for training newly arrived junior inspectors lasted nearly a year, and there was so much to learn! One of main challenges was learning some of the local Cantonese dialect (one of the most difficult languages to speak for a Westerner and indeed the world because of its eleven tones) and the particular southern Chinese customs. Not only was the language difficult, but the reserved nature of the Hong Kongers was one the most challenging experiences my father faced. He always found them to be too quiet, not expressing their true intentions, and lacking in bravery and chivalry (of course, you would expect him to make these generalisations, and comparing to what he was used to from parochial South Shields!). So not only was it difficult to understand the language and culture, but it was also difficult to be accepting and familiar with a totally different way of being and thinking. On top of this alien culture and people and the contrasting weather and climate, there was a major issue, which was a huge discomfort for all newly arrived officers.

Hong Kong is known for its heat and humidity and has a tropical climate similar to Singapore or Malaysia, but it does have seasonal weather. For six months of the year, it regularly reaches 90°C with humidity in the 90 per cent, and that for northerner, like my father, must have been hell! I am sure in those days, air conditioning was limited (unlike now, where Hong Kong has the coldest air conditioning in the world officially, and most of the locals cannot live without it!) so they had to adapt and endure a totally alien climate. The summer tropical typhoons were another condition that the newly arrived Westerners were completely unfamiliar with, and these would hit Hong Kong with ferocious winds and torrential rain. Structural damage, massive flooding, and landslides left a trail of destruction that would take weeks to clear up. The HK observatory now has a grading system of the severity of the typhoon, which ranges from Typhoon signal 1 to 10, where signal 3 warns of heavy rain and winds of up to 100 km/h. Anything beyond signal 8 or a 'black storm' of wind and rain would cause structural damage and a danger to life. When signal 8 is hoisted, then the whole of Hong Kong shuts down (most unusual), from offices to schools and banks, flights, and public transport. Signal 10 is a direct hit, which means 'in the eye of the storm', and when Hong Kong becomes a ghost town! I can recall a time when I was at school in Quarry Bay North Point and literally, the heaviness of the rain felt like turning on the shower at full blast—I was almost drowning!

Living and adapting to these extremes in climate, certainly was an eye-opener for my father, considering where he came from. There was almost guaranteed snow in the winter and mild warm summers on the North East coast of England; for my father to see and experience these tropical storms must have been quite a shock to the system. I know my father did not like the humidity one bit nor did his colleagues, and one of the more pleasant ways of cooling down was to drink more beer! (San Miguel was Father's favourite and for the next twenty years!) But as we know now, alcohol dehydrates you and makes the condition worse, yet one could understand that drinking, to a Geordie and his colleagues, was as natural as local Chinese eating rice every day. For practical working and living conditions to be more comfortable in the sapping heat and humidity was to have huge ceiling fans rotating constantly, especially in the evenings and that the police uniform in the summer allowed them to wear shorts. All of the time he was in uniform (until later in his career), the style of the Hong Kong Police was modelled on the British Army—a khaki light green with the usual hat, holster for the gun, and those heavy, thick, black army leather shoes. Having to wear those shoes all day in that heat and humidity, sometimes more than a twelve-hour shift, meant that his feet were cooking in his sweat, unable to breathe and dry out, and leaving an incredible stench! From that experience, he caught the infamous 'Hong Kong foot' virus, (a very irritating itchy fungal infection that can keep you awake at night) that was to plague him for the rest of his life. In those days, I suppose, there was not much treatment for that condition, and it was so bad that my mother could not even sleep in the same bed with him—and other reasons, much more later. Even my mother got the virus, probably from him, and I experienced the condition myself in the times I had been back!

One of the main criteria for recruiting 'fresh and eager young blood', like my father, was the serious problem of illegal immigrants coming over from 'Communist Red China'. They swam (some were eaten by sharks in the waters of the New Territories), climbed mountains, hid in dense forests, used Chinese junks and sampans (small fishing boats) to cross the waters, did night raids across border points—you name it—they tried everything! The then Hong Kong administration was getting paranoid of this mass influx of Communist Chinese that could potentially destabilise the society, or as one previous famous British Prime Minister said 'we don't want to be swamped by these people!' (*Margaret Thatcher's reference to possible mass migration of Hong Kongers to the UK, if the 1997 handover to China turned out to be a disaster*).

So my father's first posting in the police was to guard the border between Hong Kong and China at Lok Ma Chau checkpoint—not exactly his idea of a great and glamorous start to a police career! It was a remote and barren region, mountainous, with local village people that had a different dialect

(Hakka) and made communication difficult. Since it's a tropical climate, it was infested with mosquitoes in the summer and was pretty cold in the winter months—a real survival experience for him. I remember my mother saying that whenever my father patrolled the crossing, using the binoculars while observing the Chinese side, he would scowl and abuse those Chinese Red Guards and would pity them for their poverty and their pathetic-looking uniform. 'Those red b—ds don't deserve any better!' he would say.

Both sides carried guns, with my father always having his revolver in his holster. The Chinese Red Guards (People's Liberation Army) always had heavier guns, with rifles and Kalashnikov machines guns. Not only did my father not like the posting there, it was a very tense time in terms of possible conflicts at any time. My mother would tell me that my father was so looking to be off duty and get away as far as possible from the area and then head straight into town for beer and socialising. With his interest in football still fresh from the north east, he also joined the police football team and became their main goalkeeper for a number of years—and yet again, he did well and was runners-up in the final of the police league in 1954. Today, Lok Ma Chau is a major new border-crossing terminal between China and Hong Kong SAR, with thousands of people visiting relatives or doing business and is served by the Mass Transit Railway (MTR) and numerous coaches and tour operators—very efficient and enormous I might add! The promise of an exciting, challenging, once-in-a-lifetime experience of serving for Her Majesty's forces did not disappoint my father at Lok Ma Chau, and there was a lot more to come, as he was soon to find out!

With the pressure of the Mao's Communist Red Guards overthrowing the old regime and now with Guangzhou in the hands of the Red Guards, my mother and her gang of colleagues were desperate to get out. She said she had made contact with some catholic missionaries' sisters, based in Guangzhou, who were helping the poor and now the native Chinese running from the communists. They offered a way out—Macao! Although it was not their planned destination of Hong Kong, it was a Portuguese colony, which would eventually be a bridge (a Chinese metaphor) to get to Hong Kong. On the backs of compassion of the Catholic sisters, they were transported to the colony and with the belief that Jesus and the Virgin Mary had saved them! My mother was led to believe that Macao was an easier port of entry than Hong Kong, and that assumption turned out to be true. With many thousands of Chinese fleeing the mainland, the Hong Kong colonial government was concerned with the massive influx of Chinese that may swamp the colony. It was ironic that the heavily guarded border crossing at Lok Ma Chau was manned by the police, with my father contributing to locking the doors to freedom to those desperate people!

So having sheltered with the Catholic sisters and found refuge, my mother made acquaintances there (not being shy!) and quickly integrated into the Macao way of life. She never did pick up Portuguese, but she was converted to Catholicism as a way of integrating with the local Macanese. I had always wondered as to why my mother was such a strong Catholic, because it didn't seem likely from the Hong Kong experience, as it was not a place of deep religious institutions. However, what she had to learn again in preparation for Hong Kong was Cantonese, and her first exposure to this was her brief stay in Guangzhou. Although deeply appreciative to the Catholic brethren for rescuing her from the communists, my mother realised she did not want to convert to be a sister or be a part of any religious (and live like a pauper) order and so made her way out of the church. She realised that what she had learnt in Shanghai could still offer a living, albeit in foreign land.

It was at this time that she became acquainted with and was seeing a regular client either from Portugal or European decent in Macao (she never divulged the information to me) and seemed to have struck up a relationship with him with the expected outcome of becoming pregnant. This was some time in 1953, and after having had a number of risky abortions already (two to three), my mother decided to go through with the pregnancy on this one. The relationship must have been serious for her to go through with this and probably the man she was with, promised to look after her and give them a future. The only thing my mother mentioned about the man was that he was a seaman and that he was not as wild or violent as some of the other servicemen. He promised a lot but failed to deliver—my mother never saw him again as she was approaching the birth-giving time. With this awkward situation and unable to earn while being pregnant, she had to seek support. My mother then developed another relationship with a local Chinese man from Hong Kong called Jimmy, who worked as a low-level clerk in Macao. He was keener on her and offered to support her through the pregnancy and adopt the child. She was grateful and because of that, she came to appreciate this man and enter into a cohabiting lovers' life. Yet, at the back of her mind, she knew that it could not last because he was not earning enough and had limited prospects. Like many of her compatriots, everyone was looking for a gweilo as a way out of the business, a future, a passport to security, security, security!

In April 1954, my mother gave birth to a boy who turned out to have blonde and curly hair—a total shock to her and Jimmy! She was finally impregnated by a European and had become a mother to a mixed child in the Portuguese colony of Macao—quite an achievement in those days but one that was fraught with derision, discrimination, and heartache, as she was to find out in the ensuing years . . . ! It was also an event, which would change the course of my mother's life dramatically.

Even with this responsibility of another child, the lure of Hong Kong and having a future in a British colony was still prominent in my mother's mind. Since Jimmy was a native of Hong Kong, and they were confirmed lovers and partners, he was willing to sponsor my mother, get her across, and live with him in Kowloon. I am sure the offer of marriage came up from Jimmy, but knowing my mother's intention, she really wanted a Western passport and husband. My mother told me that he was a kind man, willing to be patient and hoped, that one day soon, his love for her would win her over—he was sorely disappointed as the years went by! They settled in a tiny flat in around the Tsim Sha Tsui area with Jimmy able to transfer his work back to Hong Kong side from Macao. Being a refugee from China and virtually smuggled in, my mother had no right to work and had to rely completely on Jimmy's meagre salary to support the three of them. There was another mouth to feed and the fact that she had had that liberating experience of working and fending for herself in Shanghai, she said she felt very uncomfortable and frustrated that life was still so tough, even in Hong Kong. I remember her saying 'love alone cannot provide good food, shelter, and comfort on the table'. This was her constant complaint about Jimmy. After all, one of the main reasons why she ran from the mainland was to look for a better life—in all areas! She said he had limited prospects, a future of just working as a clerk and that was all! She managed to tolerate this situation long enough until the boy was about three years old, and this is where she made another heartbreaking decision. She had found a boarding school in Macao and decided to send the boy to be looked after there, safe in the knowledge that he was born there and that the Catholic community would give him a secure upbringing—it turned out to be a disaster for the boy and for my mother as well. My mother had gotten to a state that she could no longer get by with Jimmy's meagre salary and reasoned with herself and Jimmy that she would have to go back to that business to earn a better income for all them—and support this boy's boarding school fees. I am sure Jimmy's reaction to my mother's decision was one of disapproval (he was quite a traditional Cantonese man), but the situation required some radical action. And by this time, my mother was approaching her mid-thirties, and she was not exactly young. So another desperate scenario for my mother to face and this solution had significant repercussions for her relationship to her son and Jimmy. She had already left a daughter behind in China, and now her son in Macao . . . . The decision to return to the nightlife entertainment business proved too lucrative to ignore but at a high cost, as she was to discover years down the line . . .

Still armed with the charms of femme fatale and a certain streetwise ways of the Shanghai training school for dancing bargirls, my mother was adequately prepared and self-confident enough to be quickly integrated into the Hong Kong bar scene. The only nagging concern to her was her age—she was in her early thirties. Even as a fully shaped and a sculptured dancing and bargirl schooled in Shanghai, the competition was fierce from the young pretenders (young 'Suzie Wong's') snapping at her five-inch stiletto heels! The exaggerated world of Suzie Wong painted a picture of a glamorous lifestyle—elegant, refined, silky, long black hair Chinese women in figure-hugging Cheongsam catches the eye of the rugged or sophisticated tall blond and blue-eyed Western man to the rescue! It conjured up the image of the perfect love affair of passion, adventure, excitement, and fascination—a meeting of two civilisations that represented divergent cultures and history—the old adage of 'opposites attract'. And, of course, Hollywood jumped on this fantasy to make a movie in 1960, *The World of Suzie Wong*, starring William Holden and Nancy Kwan—it was a hit. The reality, however, was quite different. In that time of history and with the world recovering from WWII, Hong Kong was infiltrated with an array of armed forces from the west, especially the Americans, Australians, and Canadians, and these servicemen were again needed to be stationed there for the start of the Korean War and the establishment of the People's Republic of China.

Hong Kong was an important port for the navy, with HMS Tamar being the central docking point for the HM's Navy. When the naval servicemen arrived to have a good time in Hong Kong, that's where the services of mother's colleagues were required. My mother and her fellow gang knew that this business offered them at least a living and perhaps a future, more security, and even perhaps 'falling in love' with a man, finding that husband and gaining the security of a foreign passport. Yet there were numerous incidents, which, my mother told me, were of gweilos arriving drunken, foul-mouthed, abusive, sometimes violent men, and having been given a good time, would then run off without paying a cent! The most generous were the Americans, and the worst were the British! With contraception virtually non-existent then, my mother recalled of so many of friends/colleagues becoming pregnant and most had to abort them. In the business they were in, abortions were carried out by dubious clinicians in the back alleys of Hong Kong, and my mother remembered an incident of a colleague who had got one done, only to find out later that she died a painful death on the steps to her apartment from infections and haemorrhaging. Fortunately, for my mother, she was one of the luckier ones not to face the same fate, although she had mentioned she had aborted on a couple of occasions. Nothing glamorous about the life of Suzie Wong!

My mother always found the Cantonese culture awkward to deal with. She was a native of Hankow Wuhan, an inland province that had little seafood except for rivers and staple diet, quite different from Hong Kong. From where she came from, she had only spoken a heavily accented Mandarin with a very pronounced Hankownese accent (I could just about understand the dialect when I travelled with her on our only visit in 1983 as young undergraduate). So one could imagine how challenging it was for her to communicate with the local Hong Kongers and their Cantonese ways and customs. As food is central to the Chinese culture, my mother was mostly used to eating noodles, buns (bao) and limited amount of rice, whereas for the Cantonese, their staple starch diet was all centred around rice. And the popular 'dim sum' was a completely new type of food she had never come across—my mother had in fact not been much of a fan of dim sum even up to her last days. Added to the fact that she hardly spoke Cantonese, and when she opened her mouth to converse, the Hong Kongers would immediately notice and comment that another refugee had arrived at their shores (she never lost her Hankow accent when I heard her speaking Cantonese). Fortunately, for my mother, she was an extrovert and socialised easily. She had already picked up Shanghainese proficiently, so learning languages was not too much of a struggle for her. Yes, there was certainly discrimination in those days, and my mother had her fair share of it! Yet the simple fact was that this was the reality she was facing—either she adapted and accepted the environment or risked starvation, isolation, and being sent back to her homeland. My mother, true to her Chinese heritage, was very pragmatic—she chose the former!

On deciding to offer her personal services again in this nightlife of Hong Kong, the strain in her relationship with Jimmy was getting more pronounced. He was working in the office, the usual nine to five routine (more eight to six Monday to Saturday in Hong Kong) and my mother worked late evenings and sometimes round the clock—there are no set timings in that line of work! So they hardly saw each other, and as for having the time for intimacy . . . no chance. Drifting apart, my mother realised it was better that she found her own place, while still wanting to maintain a friendship with Jimmy—she still had her uses from him!

'Without Jimmy, I would not have lasted in Hong Kong,' my mother said gratefully. He was her only support, yet my mother again felt trapped and suffocated by the relationship. They amicably agreed to live separately since my mother was gaining confidence living in the area and getting more used to the local Cantonese ways. She eventually found a place to stay in Mody Road. It was an ideal location as it was located around the backstreets of the main Tsim Sha Tsui area and away from the incessant traffic of Nathan Road. Bars and clubs littered the streets of Mody Road, with all the working girls living upstairs above. My mother hated living in those conditions, sometimes four in a room in bunk beds with others and having to put up with other Chinese who did not speak a word of Mandarin or were from other parts of China with different dialects, such as Fujian and Hakka. And not far from where they slept, there were the knocking shops (on the floor below), which were really whorehouses where business was conducted assiduously. She, however, did not have much choice, and she was still grateful for work and a roof over her head, making some money, and learning more Cantonese to give her more of a head start over others that were still struggling to speak the language. Added to her ability to learn languages fast and her natural extroversion in social situations, she started making a name for herself in the Tsim Sha Tsui bar areas. Yet the haunting reminder that she was hitting her mid-thirties and knowing how fickle the business was, there was always that feeling of desperation again and looking for that elusive Western lover or potential husband. She told me that had she not met a good man (preferably Western) by thirty-five, she would pack up and go back to China.

Tsim Sha Tsui was, and still is, one of the two main 24-7 nightlife areas in Hong Kong—the other being the Wan Chai district on Hong Kong side. The area was almost next door to the harbour, with established bars and restaurants in the vicinity and the famous Nathan Road shopping district to boast. Ship's personnel and all the armed forces frequented this area to look for evening entertainment, with this its exaggerated neon signs 'Red Lion Bar or Suzie Wong's' (there was an actual bar called that) enticing the new tourists. My mother settled more on the Kowloon Side because she said it was still easier to get in there, as it was the mainland part of Hong Kong, not having to cross the harbour by Star Ferry to Hong Kong side. The competition to Tsim Sha Tsui was of course Wan Chai Central District, and with HMS Tamar stationed there, it was still the central naval base and docking point for British and foreign personnel to disembark.

Wan Chai and the surrounding area turned out to quite a stalking place for both my parents and one where I had some memorable experiences with them—more later.

Being well established in and around Mody Road bar areas and mother's nickname of 'sexy fat ass' by her colleagues, a chance meeting with a lady called Mrs Khan (Auntie Khan) and 'Ah Law' was the opportunity that my mother had been waiting for! What was also very helpful to my mother as newly arrived refugee from China was that they were local Cantonese women, born and bred Hong Kong and knew all the street-wise idiosyncrasies that proved to be invaluable to my mother's survival in that city. Both Auntie Khan (she was later to marry a Pakistani Khan) and Ah Law were in the same business and had established themselves in the Tsim Sha Tsui area, and had captured a secure base of clientele to run a brothel. Auntie Khan was a little older than my mother was, probably in her late-thirties and was more a 'Mama San,' organising, running, renting, and generally managing the place. My mother said she was very grateful to Auntie Khan because she took her in and saved her from some of the more unsavoury characters running the brothels then. They became quite close friends, to the point that my mother almost treated her like an elder sister, and she was able to trust and feel safe with her in handling her clients and making sure that she was paid. There were other areas that Auntie Khan helped my mother in—from what food to eat, how to dress, to taste more dim sum and local delicacies.

It was like an initiation ceremony for my mother to enter the Cantonese clan of life. The friendship was also crucial to my mother in that she learnt and became more sophisticated in the etiquette of the Hong Kong style of doing business, which elevated her to serve a better class of clientele. The other good friend was a young and ambitious 'Ah Law', a typical Cantonese woman who was rather brash, loud, and sometimes crude, but a good heart and someone she could also trust and rely on. She was the youngest out of the three, so, in a way, she had an innocence about her that my mother liked. My mother recalled stories of Ah Law advising her to stay away from certain areas of Kowloon (Mong Kok, Yau Ma Tei, and the New Territories) for her own personal safety, as there were numerous cases of rape and kidnapping from the 'coolies' of rough areas. The threat of rival pimps and their gangs were always present, so they also used to go out together or in groups of four to five girls. Thanks to Ah Law, my mother was introduced to the game of 'Mah-jong', a popular game in southern China, which gave many people enjoyment and camaraderie around the table for four players. As long it was not playing for high stakes, it was one of the most accepted forms of gambling and a gathering where friends met and new friendships developed to gossip about their lives. The ritual of taking turns of playing each other's residence meant that they could spend the whole evening (and all through the morning sometimes) having dinner, socialising, and gave them the ideal 'chill out' place away from the pressures and demanding personal services that so dominated their lives. My mother became quite addicted to the game as years went by, and when she won, not that often, she was sweet, but when she lost . . . !

As my mother grew to be more confident and familiar with the Tsim Sha Tsui area, Auntie Khan had met and fallen in love with a Pakistani man (most unusual for Chinese to mix with Asians known locally as 'Ah Char' and in fact looked down on them!) and was considering getting out of that business. She had run a number of brothels in Mody Road, Hankow Road, and in the backstreets off that, and my mother suggested she could take over and manage the places for her. They came to some arrangement, and eventually Auntie Khan got out completely and kept a couple of apartments in Haiphong Mansions which she subsequently used for her family and the other to rent out for commercial use (actually was a small knitting and sewing firm). Haiphong Mansions is directly opposite the Kowloon Park (and later added was the Kowloon Mosque), which was obviously convenient to them as practising Muslims. The mosque now is prime real estate land in the heart of Tsim Sha Tsui and Nathan Road, but somehow the Muslim clerics and the worshippers have vowed never to sell the land to the numerous offers made from the developers over the years! Kowloon Mosque is the centre for all the Muslims in Hong Kong. When I was to visit Auntie Khan in the 1980s, she was a frail-looking woman who chain-smoked and was going downhill fast, yet she still had the spirit and mentoring influencing to advise my mother with her issues later in life (more later).

Events and changes in personal circumstances were developing fast. Gaining more in stature and making a name for herself—my mother's nickname with the other girls was 'fat bottom', which she hated—she established her place in Mody Road and started renting the rooms out to other girls for their clients. Ah Law had met a seaman from Australia and eventually fell in love and married the Australian and got her passport and so-called security. Everyone (the colleagues that she knew) was wanting to get out! That age question was rearing its ugly head again and my mother realised she had to find a way out of this business as desperation was beginning to set into daily consciousness again! All her life up until now was to look for security, understandable from where she had come from, and now, where the business had initially offered her the freedom, livelihood, and a certain amount of dignity—she felt trapped by her circumstances. The pressure was on, especially with the growing, ominous presence of the triads and gangs, which were muscling in on the trade. It was getting too dangerous (and she was too old) she said, to be involved with that kind of set up. Once you got involved with them, it was a life sentence of extortion, intimidation, and enslavement.

'No way!' my mother said.

Their First Encounter

My father had settled into his inspector's post well and had passed his probationary assessment with flying colours. His duty on the Lok Ma Chau border was commended for his commitment and professional conduct in handling a very challenging situation in that period of Hong Kong history. Apparently, I was to find out from some of my father's old colleagues that it was a deliberate tactic to station junior probationary inspectors to see if they could last the course—and many of them didn't and quit the force, while some even before the probationary period were up for review. Hardened by the border experience and having to practise his Pidgin Cantonese with the local villages around Lok Ma Chau, my father seemed to have integrated well into Hong Kong culture. It was also during that posting there, when he had built up some new friendships with colleagues that shared his Geordie sense of humour (Wy Ay Man!). My father was a proud northerner, known for straight talking, hard drinking, and boisterous behaviour, and of course, women! He avoided Brits that were from the south—that is anything south of Yorkshire—and he couldn't stand Londoners and those from South East England. He considered them to be 'snobbish southern b—ds' and saw them as lacking masculine manhood and 'a bunch of sissies'. As far as I can recall, when I met my father's friends they were all either Scottish, Irish, and from the North East and North West. However, there was one exception—a senior inspector from London, who would make international news for corruption charges. My father mentioned that he had quite a healthy respect for this man because of his vigour, bravery, and leadership qualities that he showed in managing his men under him. He was six years older than my father was, and he was surprised that a southerner could have this charisma. I think my father felt intimidated by him, not because he was afraid of him, but because of his ability. He probably knew that this infamous officer had a promising future ahead of him and would have the prospect of rapid promotion to a very high level in the police force. This officer did not disappoint—more later.

Having spent two to three years on Lok Ma Chau posting and keen to get away from the 'coolie area' of the New Territories, he was delighted to be given his next position to Hong Kong Island. I think if my father was ordered to stay on as border police he may have resigned and only serve a three-year term—how fine the line of destiny runs! Not only was he back in Hong Kong Island, but his quarters were also based above Wan Chai Police Station, just where all the action was! He had been to Wan Chai on numerous occasions before when he was off duty and went with the lads from Lok Ma Chau, but the journey from the border to downtown must have been long and arduous. The local brew San Miguel had got my father hooked, and by this time in 1955-56, he had built up a regular gang of drinking lads for them to hit the town for their all-night binges. But now, he was stationed in the heart of Hong Kong and the red-light district was just around the corner, and the access to nightlife, bars, women were at his beck and call. My mother told me that this was his first position in the city to patrol the streets of Hong Kong, on the beat, and it was a fantastic way to get to know all the areas and where the action was happening. Wan Chai

Police Station was one of the first stations to be built by the colonials, earlier in the century, with only the Central Police Station being older. It still stands quite majestically on Harbour Road today, with traffic thundering across and view of the much more diminished Hong Kong Harbour.

In those days, junior inspectors had their quarters above the larger police stations, and all of them had their individual rooms with their own cleaning and showering facilities—something like a bedsit today. Food was served in the canteen in those days, and armahs used to be hired by the police to do all the cleaning and laundry for the officers. Since their quarters were above the station, there were strict house rules they had to follow in terms of noise and times of returning when they were off duty. One of the major restrictions was that under no circumstances would female guests be allowed to visit them in their rooms—quite obvious really, this was the Wan Chai area! Hong Kong Island always had more Europeans living there than the mainland Kowloon Side, mainly due to the fact that HMS Tamar was built on the Hong Kong harbour side, and the first police station built was in Central District. So with all the service personnel based in a relatively small area, it was natural that the bars and entertainment business were located almost round the corner to serve these thirsty men. Some fifty years later, there hasn't been much change, with even more bars and clubs that serve all clients, not just servicemen.

My father was at the height of his testosterone manhood as a twenty-seven or twenty-eight years old police officer in 1956, and I am sure he took full advantage of it. At six feet two inches fit and slim (still the police force's first choice goalkeeper) he must've looked impressive in uniform to the ladies, whether they came from the street or not. My mother told me that the first car my father had was a huge American Lincoln Continental which he was so proud of, and this was a privilege that he could only dream of if he was still in the north-east—he didn't complain about it being American, he owned a car! With his beat in the heart of Hong Kong and all the temptations of nightlife, exotic oriental women, and that faithful San Miguel, he was living the life that a lot of his colleagues back home in England could only see on the silver screen or read in an exotic novel—the world of 'Suzie Wong' was real!

Hong Kong was still undergoing a period of reconstruction in the mid-1950s, and the disaster of the Shek Kip Mei fire among the squatter huts in 1953, rendered 50,000 people homeless. Governor Grantham, in response to the crisis, embarked on an emergency public housing scheme to give shelter to these desperate people. According to my mother, my father remarked that he did not realise that the majority of local Hong Kong people lived like this and that they (the government) should do something about it. A lot of these people were refugees and economic migrants from the mainland, and the government had a policy of not feeding or housing the destitute for fear of encouraging more mass migration from China. However, once the emergency relief had ended, the governor was under pressure to do more to give shelter. This initiative was to be followed up by a massive resettlement programme, which till today in Hong Kong is housing millions of local people in high-rise public housing—ugly but efficient. From this, a comprehensive welfare programme was established for the first time in Hong Kong's history. In parallel to the housing scheme, the government introduced a rudimentary but efficient and universal health service for a nominal charge, which could be waived for the poor. Added to this was the offer of free public education to the masses.

So, for my father, enjoying his stint as a young inspector in an exclusive part of Hong Kong contrasted vastly to the near poverty and destitute conditions of a larger part of the population. He did say that the divide between the rich and poor reminded him of parts of the UK (he mentioned Durham as the affluent part of the North East), but the differences were starker in Hong Kong. Squatter huts are desperately basic and fragile—mainly made of rusting corrugated iron thrown together to make a roof and the four walls as a hut. Sewerage and water supply were standpipes in the streets, and electric supply was irregular and primitive. I recall, as a young school boy in North Point, walking through the streets and seeing the locals shacked up into makeshift accommodation, sometimes five to six in one room, living room/dining and sleeping in bunk beds. With the extremes of a tropical climate and the unbearable heat and humidity, conditions must have been atrocious. Once the typhoon season hit, the wind and rain would sometimes devastate the area. I am not surprised that the great squatter hut fire in 1953 shook up the colonial government. Now I can understand why the government had to start a massive construction programme to house these people, and even today there are pockets of substandard living conditions in Hong Kong. Even though they are ugly, the towering blocks of public housing that dominate the skyline today, have served its purpose and provided safe and healthy living conditions that the locals appreciate.

As an officer on the beat, my father was able to see the reality behind the deceptive temptations of Wan Chai and Tsim Sha Tsui—I remember his direct but compassionate words 'those poor Chinese b—ds!' He knew he was lucky like most of the gweilos of his generation.

Cruising around Hong Kong with the Lincoln must have been quite a challenge on Hong Kong's narrow streets. With all that chrome and fenders, and at the time when rock 'n' roll (Bill Haley and the Comets, Elvis Presley) exploded on to the radio waves, it must have been an exciting and interesting time to be living in. That era was one of regeneration, renewal, and rediscovery, and after the trauma and misery of WWII, the 'joie de vivre' attitude that emerged seemed to want to celebrate a new beginning for society. My father was never a fan of Elvis (my mother said he was jealous of Elvis's pretty boy American looks) and preferred the more laid-back Frank Sinatra. He wasn't a dancer either on the floor, preferring to watch from the bar all that jiving and swing that was so fashionable in those days. I remember my mother saying that my father was a shy man in most social situations and only became boisterous, loud, and daring once he was fully loaded with his San Miguel—quite English, I suppose. My mother, on the other hand, loved dancing, thanks to the Shanghai school of bars and dance halls that she so revelled in (something that I inherited too, especially rock 'n' roll jiving) and this was probably one of her most attractive traits to lure clients. As he was getting familiar with the bar area of Wan Chai and Central, his friends and colleagues were also told of the Tsim Sha Tsui area of Kowloon Side that was just as fun and exciting. From the station at Wan Chai, in that time one could see the full view of the harbour, the mainland of Kowloon, and the regular crossing of the Star Ferry boat that carried people between the two places. It was quite a novelty for Westerners to use the ferry, but also there was no harbour tunnel built then for any vehicle to drive across. The Star Ferry was the only way to get across! My father had been to Tsim Sha Tsui a few times when he was posted at Lok Ma Chau, but now this was the first time that he had to use the ferry to get across from central—and it was cheap and convenient. So on the rest days, which could be any day in the week, my father and his bunch of lads would cruise the bars of Mody Road, Chatham Road, and the surrounding streets to start their evening.

My mother was already set up in her comfortable but compact apartment in Mody Road. She was managing to run the place that housed a few other women in the trade, and now she was established as a 'Mama San' in her right. From there my mother was able to work in the area, and allowances were made to be able to bring clients back for them to do their business. She was still in a relationship with Jimmy, but there was an understanding between them that this working arrangement had to be maintained to be able to maintain her living standards and also for paying her son's school fees in Macao. My mother said she felt guilty on both fronts—having to almost abandon him to a boarding and depriving him of an upbringing from a parent, and her growing separation with Jimmy. On vacation breaks, the boy would come back to Hong Kong and stay with her, and during that time, Jimmy and the boy would develop almost a father/son relationship. After all, he was the only male figure around. Jimmy had been so close to the boy that he offered to adopt him, but for some reason my mother did not accept that from him. With hindsight, and my mother agreed years later, that it would have been the best outcome for the boy that she should've let Jimmy adopt him and bring him up—at least he was a willing parent and that he would be there for him. The type of man Jimmy was, as she described him to me, was of a highly dedicated nature and one who was truly loyal—the best traits of Chinese morals. Jimmy's view was 'if I can't have you, then at least I have something that comes from you!'

Being fond of dancing and not shy in expressing her talents, my mother said the best part of her work was dancing with a partner or a client that could dance—and there weren't too many that could! She said that after her dance sessions, she would rest at the bar and join the client for a drink, and from there, she would either engage with the client or move on to another one. She would not tolerate too many time-wasters! My mother was working in a bar on Hankow Road (what a coincidence) in 1957-58, and it just so happened that my father was a regular drinker there. Almost everybody smoked in those days, a status symbol of some wealth, and out of the misty smoky ambience with the live band thumping out a jive beat, they first lay their eyes on each other. My mother recalls that she had noticed my father before at the bar, drinking with his colleagues and friends, and that's all they did! She always commented that my father never took to the dance floor—and he wasn't a keen dancer. It was a number of weeks before she finally got the opportunity to approach my father on his own, as it was difficult for her to break in when he was in a group of three to four men round the bar. But when the opportunity came, the sparks flew! One of the first gestures of getting to know him was when my mother invited him to dance; he declined straight away for fear of 'making a fool of himself', in my mother words. I am sure the way in which how confidently my mother moved on the dance floor with her classic glass-shaped figure would attract many clients, not only my father! I can imagine how the both of them would've interacted, probably rather basic as he was neither fluent in Cantonese or Mandarin, and she was struggling with her Pidgin English. Yet, the attraction and sexual chemistry was there, and they 'hit it off pretty quickly', as my mother reminisced. She said that one the reasons she was attracted to him was not only because he was handsome and had the stature to go with it, but also because other girls, who had some contact with him, commented on his gentlemanly ways and on his being quite polite in manner. It was only after a few drinks (as usual) that he would start going into another state, and then she saw another side to the man. But my mother was intensely drawn to him and vice versa, and in a world with so much temptation for the gweilo, my father had plenty of choices to go for, and yet as fate would have it, he was drawn to make his choice for my mother.

Once they had established that rapport with each other, my mother said that my father kept coming back to the same bar every week. Of course, it led to the physical relationship quite early on (on the second or third meeting, my mother says), but this time it was something different for her. Every time my mother would be on her shift, she would be on the lookout for my father, knowing that as police, he worked irregular shift patterns and was unable to know when he would show up. And in those days of primitive communications, telephones were few and far between. Within six months of their first encounter, they had both cemented a relationship that was more than a girl/ client set-up. As my mother had her own private apartment in Mody Road, it was ideal for my father to visit her when they wanted to spend time together, and this especially so, since he was still based at Wan Chai station police single men's quarters. The relationship was getting deeper and stronger, and according to my mother, my father did not want her to go out with any other man—was he getting jealous? She felt that same way too, and all the philandering was both making them uneasy and lacking in purpose. Yet, being the usual pragmatic Chinese, she had to continue doing this as this was her livelihood, and it was the only skill she possessed.

It was early 1958, and now they had been together solidly for six months, with my father still having the Lincoln Continental cruising around Hong Kong with my mother by his side. My mother had never been in a private car before, especially driven by a man she adored, and these were the moments she treasured. They cruised round Hong Kong, of course, and one of the special highlights for my mother was driving up to the Peak district and seeing the splendid view of the harbour—up to that time she had not even been across to the island! It was at the Peak restaurant during candlelit dinners and drinks (of course!) where my father would romance and serenade her. Harry and Vicky (my mother took to the name Victoria from Victoria Park) were falling in love! Was he the man she had been looking for all her life? Was this the love that would give her security, stability, and passion, which was so desperately missing in her world? Was he the man that she wanted to marry and have a family with that she could truly call her own?

My father was in competition with another Westerner for my mother's affections. She had already befriended an American serviceman in the bar who also offered my mother a future of marriage and security in the US. Being the usual pragmatic Chinese, my mother said one the crucial factors that swayed her choice in favour of my father was the fact that he was based in Hong Kong and that his position in the police force was more secure than this American sailor. My father had mentioned to her that his contract with Hong Kong Police Force would be for a minimum of ten years—and that did the trick! So not only was it deep passion and sexual chemistry between them that brought them together, but also the hard reality of having the 'iron rice-bowl'—security for life for a Chinese refugee like my mother which turned out to be the dominant factor in choosing Harry Craggs.

Having made her decision for Harry, my mother said that she made the right choice. In that blissful time of encapsulating passion and love and the era of the 1950s, their world was joyful and beautiful—almost like in the film—*The World of Suzie Wong*, made in 1960. The film which starred William Holden and the little-known Nancy Kwan (of mixed raced) tells of a story of an American artist who arrives in Hong Kong and becomes fascinated with the culture and the backstreet life of the city. He meets a dancing girl called 'Suzie Wong', and they fall in love.

It has been many years since I saw the film, and as part of my research I thought it was important for me to see the film again to see if it had any correlation to my mother's life and how both my parents met in Hong Kong—I was not disappointed! The message I got from the film was of a woman who was desperate to get out the vice world (like my mother) and find true love with man that would offer her a secure future (same as my mother). To complicate things even further for *Suzie*, she bears a child and raises it by herself after the father has abandoned the both of them and hides it (as in the birth of half-brother before my mother met my father). Overall, *Suzie* is portrayed as pragmatic and realistic and guards her principles and character forcefully. Yet as the film probes a little deeper into her world, it shows *Suzie* as a woman with a kind heart and has hopes and dreams of a better life (my mother again).

My mother recalls affectionately that every time my father would visit her in the apartment, he would arrive at the door in his pristine police officer uniform, tall and elegant with an air of authority and demeanour and shining black shoes that glistened in the hallway lights. He would stand there, as if to attention, and extend the offering of a bouquet of fresh flowers. When she would open the door, he would say, 'Hello, Vicky!

This is for you.' He would say this with a charming and cheeky smile on his face, my mother remembers affectionately. It was the first time, in her hard life, that a man was offering such a gesture of love and affection that captured my mother's heart. Yet, the image of an authoritarian figure in uniform representing strength and power was so finely counterbalanced by the gift of flowers, which portrayed such a sweet and subtle scenario of their relationship—quite enchanting!

One memorable story that my mother told me was of my father who would always be extremely grateful to her was about the time when he thought he had lost his gun. As uniformed officers, and on the beat, the police carried handguns. One of the cardinal rules was that if the officer loses it other than using it on duty, it would mean an instant dismissal from the force and massive humiliation for him. The thought of losing his job and having to return to the UK absolutely terrified him! My mother described the absolute panic and sheer trauma that he was going through in trying to find the gun, sweating profusely, pacing up and down her apartment, ashen-faced with terror and worrying that his gun had really disappeared for good. Eventually my mother found it for him—it was left in the bedroom cupboard in her room after one his numerous overnight stays with her. She said that when she found it for him, he completely let his guard down and showed his appreciation. She saw the 'love in his eyes, like almost a kind gentle glow in his face', as she described it then. There were many other episodes of tenderness, affection, and passion that existed between them, yet my mother recalled these as the most memorable moments only towards the end of her life.

Even her colleagues and rivals in the business could notice that something or someone had captured my mother's attention. Ah Law and another local

Cantonese girl called Rita (Auntie Rita) started teasing her that she was falling for this Harry. They had had brief interactions with him as well, but purely out of business, but they did not have the same chemistry as my mother had with him. Also, it was one of the classic rules that girls should not get romantically involved with their clients. My mother was warned by Ah Law and Rita that Harry had a real drinking problem, and when he had had quite a few beers, he was not so much of a gentleman. Of course, my mother was blinded by this love and chose to ignore the advice (unfortunately true). She continued to get involved with Harry. It must have been difficult for her to keep this secret affair going and yet having to still serve other clients. Yet my mother said that every time my father visited the bar, he would ask for Vicky, and only for Vicky. The secret was out—they were a couple! I suspect the other girls and friends had a touch of jealousy in them as well, since they were looking for their 'Prince Charming' to rescue them out of the world of vice and live in a more secure place. Yet, the locals, according to my mother, had frowned upon and 'looked down' on Chinese women who had any idea of going for mixed marriages. It was fine to have them as boyfriends and lovers, but to marry them . . . ! (It was not only the British who practised racial discrimination; the Chinese had their own ways). Her friends would say 'these gweilos are unreliable. They smell. They are dirty and are often violent. They play around too much'! Yet, my mother, being her independent self and having a 'couldn't care less attitude' about what others thought of her, followed her heart. Besides, she said, 'I'm not one of those local Hong Kong people anyway!' There were a few other rebels like Auntie Rita and Ah Law who stood out from the crowd, and I suppose that's why my mother became friends with them. Auntie Rita eventually found her man Stanley, another police inspector originally from

Lancashire, and pretty soon, all three of them (Vicky, Ah Law, Rita) were in relationships with their prized gweilo partners. My mother said that all of them felt uplifted and more relaxed about working in the bars because now they had something more secure and an emotional support that gave them strength and patience. She even said that they became even more attractive to their clients and were doing better business! (I don't think my father or the other men would've approved, though!)

However, beneath the romance and the passion, their relationship had some lingering stark realities and past issues for both my parents. For my father, with some six years service behind him and a promise of a bright future in the force, he still had the nagging guilty feeling of having fathered a child that he had left behind in South Shields. There were hardly any long-distance telephone calls in those days, but letters were exchanged between my father and his mother, Nana, and sister, Mable. My mother told me later that my father used to be really upset about this, and that his family would make him feel so 'ashamed and a coward' for not facing his responsibility of being a father to this child. All this really hurt him, because he was a proud Geordie man! And yet even though he was thousands of miles away from his hometown, falling in love with a Chinese woman being an inspector in the police, the 'emotional blackmail' heaped on him from them haunted him in all the years in Hong Kong. According to my mother, he never forgave Nana and Mable up until his death.

For my mother, it was even more complicated. Jimmy was still around as a friend/ex-lover, and the boy would stay with her when the school had holiday breaks. There was also the matter of her daughter See Yee in China, but that was something way back that would not bother her future life in Hong Kong and with Harry. So both of them had baggage of past relationships, and my mother waited to see how the relationship developed before revealing to my father that she had this boy to look after and Jimmy in the background. Quite clearly, the relationship had become strong enough over time, and it was arranged by my father to meet the boy at my mother's apartment. My mother said my father related quite well to the boy and had a fun time playing with him every time he came to visit them at Mody Road. According to my mother, he took to the boy quite well (to make a good impression to my mother) and even took the three of them out for a day. Sensing that my father was so accommodating and understanding, Jimmy was introduced to him as my mother's 'good friend' and someone that helped her a lot. Almost everything was out in the open on my mother's side, but my father kept his own hometown issues to himself and did not share with my mother until years later in the relationship. As far as my mother was concerned, Harry was her man and someone she wanted to be with for the future, and Jimmy got the message. Once that was dealt with, it was only a matter of time before they took things one stage further—marriage.

Patience was not one of my mother's strengths! Since everything was going well and that they made no secret of their committed relationship, she started wondering when that next step would happen. By this time, she was approaching her thirty-seventh birthday, pretty advanced for a Chinese lady and wanting desperately to get out of the business. Hong Kong's economy was growing rapidly and so was its population, and with greater development and wealth, there was more competition in every area of life. Tsim Sha Tsui, Wan Chai, and the main shopping areas of Mong Kok were bustling with trade and so was organised crime—the triads. I never knew whether my mother was directly or indirectly linked to the triads, but she did say that she was constantly being hassled by them to join them or at least pay protection money. After all, her apartment was in Mody Road, one of the hottest places to be in for evening entertainment. My father was certainly aware of this since in his patrol of the Wan Chai area and patrolling those places, he came face to face with the underworld society and probably he had first experience of seeing how they operate. My father did say to my mother that they were highly organised, extremely loyal to their own, and was impressed how they looked after the local community, as long as they paid their protection money! In a strange kind of way, my father respected them immensely and accepted them as part of Hong Kong society. I am sure my mother shared with my father the problem of these gangs, and he did sympathise with her predicament. He too was reaching an age where he thought about settling down as he was approaching his thirty-second birthday. He believed that it was the right time to commit to this relationship permanently. Besides, if he did go down that route, it would give the perfect excuse and reason to get away from all those people in South Shields and move on with his life.

It was one day, my mother said, after they had made love, she voiced her concerns to my father about her future when he suddenly said, 'Come on, Vicky, I'm going to marry you, you bloody fool!' Those words must have sounded like a music from heaven to my mother, and she said she was more relieved than elated. But there was one condition—that the son she was looking after would not be part of their future. On the one hand, she had finally got what she wanted, a new lease of life, permanently away from the vice world, and to then be disappointed that her boy could not be part of their unit—another situation for a difficult choice. There were various reasons my father did not want to take on the boy, some were financial, some professional, but knowing his pride and dignity, he wanted to start afresh and have his own family with her. My mother told me that although he was secure in his inspector post (there was a new contract to sign every four years); his actual earnings were less than my mother's. So things were tight in the beginning for him, but what he lacked in cash was made up in benefits of the job—apartment, free medical, subsidised transport, and fully paid vacation leave. If he progressed well in the job, then promotion, greater remuneration, and benefits would follow and therefore a better quality of life ensured. My mother understood his reasons for not accepting the boy (he was the old-fashioned type that would start his own family when he was ready) and she accepted the arrangement that this boy would be sent back to boarding school in Macao. Again, Jimmy offered to help and arranged with my mother that the boy could stay with him when he came to Hong Kong on school holidays. It was no wonder that Jimmy and the boy had almost developed into a father-son relationship—it should've happened and would've saved a lot of grief for everyone in the future!

Charles Henry (Harry) Craggs had finally made the proposal to marry Vicky Victoria Ng Hung. They married in the Kowloon registry office in October 1958, having known each for less than two years. Again, I discovered later from my mother that she was six years older than my father, meaning that she was born in 1922. I asked her why she lied about her age, and she replied that it was not acceptable for an older Chinese woman to marry a younger gweilo man. It was considered unlucky for the marriage and that she would be seen by her peers as using the man rather than it being a union of true love. Knowing my mother, and how pragmatic she was about her life, this was a minor issue. The more pressing issue, she told me, was whether she would still be able to have children with my father at the age of thirty-six! There was a wave of similar marriages, which my mother knew of, between her friends and colleagues, to English expatriate officers, the main ones being Rita to Stan, and another Shanghai friend, Mimi to Charlie. According to my mother, the registry ceremony was a pretty simple and basic one with just a few friends and colleagues from the both of them, but the one significant guest invited was the best man at the occasion, Jimmy.

Apparently, my father and Jimmy became quite well acquainted with each other, but not that well acquainted so as to be drinking friends! My mother said that Jimmy accepted the offer in recognition of the fact that they were no longer a couple and that my father would be able to provide for her and possibly her boy in the future. Being a typical local Cantonese man, he put on a brave face and played the part of best man with dignity, but my mother did mention that underneath that facade was a man that was greatly disappointed in love and feeling unappreciated for all that he had done for them. You could say that he was a 'spurned lover', and later he became embittered and resented my mother for what had happened. He still wanted to look after the boy and not send him back to Macao but somehow my mother insisted that the boy should stay at the boarding school. With my mother having the final say as the single parent, Jimmy faded into the background and eventually found another partner to marry. Years later, my mother did say that he wanted no more contact with any of them and left my mother's life for good.

Now that they were officially a married couple, she was entitled to a British passport—so she thought! I still have the original papers handed down to me to see that my mother was declared a citizen of a British Dependent Territory under the British Nationality Act of 1948. However, this did not mean that she was British Citizen or have a British Passport unless my father officially applied for one, which he did not do until years later. As for my mother, she was just glad that she was married to an expatriate and could envision a future with a Western man, who would offer security and a quality of life that she could experience. She felt that she had achieved her dream. Following the procedure of British Colonial regulations, once an officer of HM Forces and Overseas Civil Servant, which included the HK Police, was married, he was entitled to be allocated married quarters suitable for family, living in a secure neighbourhood and comfortable-sized apartments (we always had at least three bedrooms and even a spare room for the armah). This was excellent news for both my parents because not only did it give better accommodation, better area to live in, but it was also virtually rent-free and would be fully furnished at a minimal cost to my father. It also gave my mother a new status symbol—wife of an English officer, Western standard of living, and an opportunity to mix with higher-status women who did the same thing. You could say she was showing off, and she was, considering her background. She said that once she married Harry, she would leave those 'bitches' of old friends behind (except for a couple) and totally wipe out the memories of that sordid and demeaning work that she had been involved in for the last ten years. She was now Mrs Vicky Craggs—wife of a gweilo 'Bong Ban' (a police officer)!

They were able to move to married quarters to an apartment for officers called Grand Court, now over in Kowloon Side. The boy had been sent back to Macao, Jimmy was out of her life, and now they were living together as a happy couple, even though my father's drinking was still out of hand at times. Since everything was going quite well in this blissful period of married life, by Christmas 1958, my mother announced to my father that she was pregnant—and that was me! My mother was surprised that she could get pregnant again, considering she had already had quite a few abortions behind her and that she was approaching thirty-eight years of age. Yet, knowing my mother, she used her feminine instincts, knowing that bringing another human being into marriage would further consolidate the marriage. However, when my mother announced to my father that she was pregnant, she said that he was totally shocked and dismayed at the news. He made some excuse that he was not ready to become a parent and that the financial position they were in was not strong enough to maintain a family.

My mother was deeply disappointed. She thought that the love they shared at that time was deep enough to be able to celebrate me being born into this world (I am assured by my mother that I was born out of love and not just through sex). She saw another side to Harry that shook her favourable impression of the man. Surely, she had thought that this man was sincere in marrying her and maybe wanted to raise a small family? All through the pregnancy, my mother struggled with the thought of having another abortion, and she worried about whether this development would stress my father and damage the relationship. I suppose the problems back home were still weighing on his mind and also he was getting quite addicted to the San Miguel. As more time went by with the pregnancy, my mother still hoped that he would change and accept being a father and be happy about that. I am sure my father even sank a few more beers sobering up to the thought that marrying this Chinese woman and getting her pregnant was a serious situation he was in. As it turned out, to my mother's relief, my father did still want to commit to the marriage and had genuine feelings for her, so I was spared the abortion and was brought into this world on 25 September 1959. I was born right in the heart of Mong Kok District, and I made my first cry for life in Kowloon Hospital without any complications.

My father was there at the time of my birth, and, to my mother's pleasant surprise, he was absolutely delighted and proud to be a father—and this experience was one that he wanted. My mother mentioned that he was very happy at my birth. She said, 'Your silly father bought cigars for everyone in the maternity unit as a celebration of the birth of his son, named Peter.'

According to my mother, some of the nurses laughed at my father for giving cigars to women—saying in their Cantonese slang and describing my father as a typical 'saw gweilo'(silly white man) while giggling and chuckling amongst themselves. There aren't many boys in the Craggs family (I am the last surviving male from my father side), and according to my mother, bearing the first child as a boy was something that my father felt particularly proud of.

Looking back and trying to understand the society they were living in those times, I wondered whether it crossed my father's mind that having a son of mixed Anglo-Chinese race would trouble him. After all, during that period of Hong Kong, there were few instances of expatriates tying the knot with Chinese women. That concern was dispelled pretty quickly by my father in that I was given a Christian name, registered under British law, and as my father did say determinedly to my mother, 'My boy is British and will learn to speak only English and go to an English school. He won't have to learn any of that Cantonese nonsense!' They say that when a couple has children, this can either make the relationship stronger or can destroy it. I found it comforting when my mother told me years later that my arrival into my father's life then was an occasion that he cherished, and it also helped consolidate the marriage further—at least for the first few years.

Now that we were officially a family of three, my father was entitled to apply for family quarters and was successful in securing one in the district where he worked. This was even bigger than a married apartment, with at least three bedrooms, en suite master bedroom a balcony, and a spare room for the armah, where she could have her own privacy and actually live with us full-time. It was quite common for Chinese wives of police officers to hire an armah, and this my mum followed without hesitation to help with post-pregnancy support. Financially my parents could afford it and made life a lot easier for my mother to handle motherhood and living an English style of life. There were vanity reasons as well for the wives to have hired help, because, as my mother mentioned once, after pregnancy, they all wanted to get back their figure and retain their attractiveness to their husbands. There was still a lot of temptation out there in nightlife of Hong Kong even if the husbands were married, and quite a few of my father's colleagues were having extramarital affairs. The world of Suzie Wong was very much alive and in fact expanding and becoming quite a well-known attraction for tourists to visit.

Family Life and the 1960s Era

Hong Kong was growing fast. From economic, social, and political development, the colonial administration was allowing the local Hong Kongers more freedom to find their identity separate from the PRC across the border. With a natural deep-water port, flexible workforce, and more manufacturing being established there, prosperity was beginning to reach all levels of society. The Hong Kong Police Force was still recruiting more junior inspectors from the UK, offering them four-year contracts on running, assuming they performed competently in their probationary period. It was getting a reputation in the East as a 'highly professional, organised, and respectable job' that the local people looked up to. My father had now been in the job for nearly ten years, and he was still an inspector. Some of his compatriots had already been promoted to senior inspector and few to chief inspector. My mother recalled that he was getting resentful and jealous that those he considered less capable than himself were getting higher up the career ladder, and my mother could only guess why he was not promoted. She did say that my father was essentially an 'honest cop', someone who took pride in his work and did not want to get involved with some 'dirty tricks' as she called them. One example that she told me was that police officers were able to supervise driving lessons to the public (there were no driving schools back then) in order for them to pass the test. It was something of overtime work that officers could do to earn extra money, which my father took up on some weekends. On one occasion, the student offered my father 'black money' to make sure he could pass the test, and he accepted the money. However, when he returned home, my father was so nervous about taking the money that he stuffed the notes in his police hat in order to hide it! He showed it to my mother when he got home, and he was perspiring profusely. His hands were shaking like a leaf. My father said he wouldn't do it again as it was too risky, but my mother told me, 'Your father was a stupid fool. Everybody was doing it and even for more money!' I suppose, I shouldn't have been too surprised that my mother could encourage my father to take such bribe money, coming from where she had come from.

Corruption and bribes were beginning to set in strongly in the force as a result of greater prosperity in Hong Kong. My mother said that she could not understand as to why he wasn't able to get a promotion, but I suspect that it was a combination of factors. Being a proud Geordie, he didn't like the ploys that others would 'suck up to their superiors' and do anything or turn a blind eye to suspect procedures. He was not a 'yes man'. He also couldn't tolerate those 'southern b—ds' that he had to work with, and more of them were getting into senior positions very rapidly. Also, I imagine that when my father drank; he could not keep his mouth shut about what was going on in the force. And because he was frustrated that he would not get a promotion, he would drink more to calm himself down—a vicious circle! Or maybe he was not that capable after all, something I will never know. As in all jobs and professions, the old adage says 'it's not what you know but who you know' that gets you ahead in life. Having connections within the expatriate community was not only an advantage—it was essential for your survival and progression.

My mother was getting more concerned about the heavy drinking my father was still continuing with. She was worried for the future, and rightfully thought that as a father now and that with me in his life as his first son, to quote my mother's words 'he would change'. She was wrong! After the promise of his first term in the force, he was getting sidelined and impeded for promotion, which, in turn, led to heavier drinking and now problems with the marriage. It must have been difficult for my father to communicate his feelings to my mother about his frustration because my mother's English was not that fluent in those early days. Despite all the problems, my mother recalled that they were still very much in love with each other and because of this they could overcome these challenges. I suppose having a son detracted my father from his problems for a while and made him feel that there was life besides work, and having this person in his life gave him something to look forward to in the future. The love for me and for his Chinese wife, Vicky, was the most important thing in his life—at least for a brief period!

My mother recalled that when I was approaching a year old, my father would return home early to be with me rather than drinking into the late hours in the officer's mess—he was proud to be a father! This was reassuring and comforting to my mother. Just when he was getting used to fatherhood, another shock announcement was going to be made to my father again—my mother was pregnant again! His reaction this time was not so much of dismay but of acceptance that they were consciously creating a family, a further confirmation that they were committed to each other. In fact, my mother was shocked that she could become pregnant again at nearly forty years old! My mother probably thought that if a son can change some of his drinking habit, a second child would help even more. Unfortunately, it didn't—my father was addicted to San Miguel. In March 1961, a daughter was born to Harry and Vicky, my younger sister.

Now the Craggs family was the 'ideal' unit of four: one boy and one girl. My mother said that my father did write or telephone Nana and Mable back in South Shields to let them know that he really was moving on with his life, and the niggling issue of Audrey and her alleged child was no longer part of his life. However, Nana was surprised but delighted that she had become a grandmother and mentioned to my father that she would love to see us children. One of the attractive benefits that were introduced to officers in the 1960s was that once they had completed a four-year term, they were entitled to go on leave for six months, on full pay, tickets and travel back to the UK, paid by the Hong Kong government. Six months on full pay and everything paid for—where in the world would you have got those benefits from an employer in that time or even today? My father had been away from the UK for ten years, so it was an opportune time to have a trip back and bring home his new wife and children. For my mother, this was almost a dream come true, her first-ever overseas trip out of the Far East! My father had apparently warned my mother about Nana as a 'busy body and a crafty old woman' and that she may face some strange reactions and have difficulty in understanding them. According to my mother, she was just totally excited and was looking forward to flying for the first time in her life to a distant land and culture.

I was only two years old and my sister six months when we all flew by BOAC to London around the Christmas period of 1961. Of course, I don't remember the trip, but my mother said that my father was so responsible and felt proud of the family unit that he had created. When they arrived at London, she recalled feeling the cold and snowy conditions of the city (she was used to snow in Hankow), seeing the array of old architectural building that somehow reminded her of her time in Shanghai's Bund district. According to my mother, my father could not wait to get out of London, and having spent a few days in a London hotel, we made our way to Kings Cross Station to take the train to Newcastle upon Tyne.

We were met at the station by Mable and her husband, Jimmy, and this is the first time the other side of the Craggs family had set their eyes on a Chinese woman with two children of mixed race. One can imagine the fascination and curiosity on both sides! The stay was a delight, according to my mother, and they seemed totally to accept her into the family. Nana could not get over how lovely we were as her grandchildren and that her son Harry would be such a loving and dedicated father. Whatever issues, which still divided them (and there still were) were now totally overshadowed by this happy occasion and the new additions to the family. I sympathised with my poor mother who was just about getting by in conversational English with her husband and now had to communicate and understand the incomprehensible Geordie accent and also the strong Scottish accent of Nana. As far as my mother was concerned, out of all the of three 'on leave' trips back to the UK, this one, she said, was the happiest. Everyone was glad to see each other; there were new grandchildren in the family and to have someone like my mother to be part of these north-east folks was sheer fascination and novelty for them. My mother recounts some lovely stories of getting used to life in South Shields. The aroma of the English roast dinners had my mother salivating at the mouth, but it was the chips shops, which attracted my mother's taste buds the most. She recalled with total delight the time when she first went to a local fishand chip shop with my father in the Westoe area of South Shields and saw these giant ovens or frying machines that cooked and served the food over a counter. My mother described to me how fascinated she was to see the servers dip the fish in this milky soup substance (batter) and they would, by hand, gently drop the fish into a compartment that was filled with oil. She was even more impressed with the baskets of freshly cut potatoes that were shaped like wedges (chips) and they would be poured into another compartment full of boiling oil, which would make a 'delightful splash and crackle sound of frying', to quote her words. She said seeing the golden coloured fish lifted out of the fryer and laid on a stack of paper to be followed by copious amounts of chips sprinkled over the fish was a sight that she would never forget. Adding salt and vinegar to the fish and then being wrapped into some serving paper made the aroma irresistible, my mother recalls. She wondered why the chip shops' windows were all steamed up, and she figured out later that this was caused by the heat from the cooking, as the temperature outside was pretty cold. It was also a place where the locals could warm themselves up while they were waiting for their food.

The Sunday roast for the family was just as pleasant for her, in seeing that everyone was seated smartly at the table, with their individual plates and served with own portions. She had been so used to the Chinese way of everyone eating from the same dish, and table manners were rather crude, to say the least. On the other hand, my mother amused Nana and Mable with the use of chopsticks, which they had never seen been used in front of them before and thought they were used for a game! In fact, my mother said they had never eaten Chinese food before. My mother said she demonstrated how to use chopsticks in eating fish and chips, delicately picking individual chips on their own, and also showing how to prise open the fish to eat. They all tried, with fingers everywhere and sticks flying all over the place, and eventually they gave up. Mable just used the chopstick, poked into the chip and fish, and ate it! Nana said amusingly, 'You could use the chopstick and smack someone who was rude or misbehaved on the table.' They all bellowed with laughter. Years later, my mother said she really felt accepted by Nana as her daughter-in-law and vice versa, since my mother really did miss having a mother figure in her childhood. My father's sister, Mable, was pleasant enough but reserved judgement as to how accepting she was of this new sister-in-law. Although Nana was delighted to see her son, Harry, she did warn my mother about his drinking habit, and about how he would misbehave and become quite nasty with his language and attitude. My mother had seen glimpses of it already, but assured Nana that it was under control and that he would behave better now that he was a father of two children—a nice try by my mother!

Six months leave was a long time to be away from work. It was too long a break for my father as it turned out later, and my mother would eventually miss the bustle and adrenalin of Hong Kong. She said she really started to miss eating Chinese food and rice and all the other dishes! The experience of Spohr Terrace, South Shields, Nana, and the Geordie way of life left an indelible mark on my mother' more pleasant memories—alas for her too few!

On the return to Hong Kong from leave, my father was moved again and posted to Sai Ying Pun Western Police Station. Whether he requested the move or not isn't known, perhaps it would have given him a better chance of promotion than other postings. The early 1960s was a time of baby rearing with the assistance of a number of armahs, and the first signs of strain in the marriage between my parents. With over ten years experience in the force, my father was still in his inspector rank, and I would imagine still pretty frustrated. 'Happy Harry', the name by which my father was known to his colleagues was not that happy in reality, and he was sinking more amounts of the local brew! There were more arguments between them, probably over his heavy drinking, financial pressure with more mouths to feed, and the cost of living in the city rising in tune with its development. The strain for my mother was intense because she had to totally rely on my father for all expenses—whereas before she was independent and able to make money herself. As with all wives of police husbands, my mother was now known as a *gar tai tai*, a madam, where she didn't have to work, cook, or clean for the husband. The armah took care of all that, and with all that spare time my mother had, she would spend mornings and afternoons having 'yum cha or mah-jong games' with other Chinese police wives who she knew in the neighbourhood. Besides what else could they do, and this was an opportunity for women to gossip about each other's husband and to 'show off to each other' on how well they were doing. To the Chinese 'saving face' was one of the most important features of a person's dignity, but, according to my mother, it was exaggerated and abused to such an extent that after a point she found it intolerable. She said a lot of the Chinese wives would gossip and proclaim how wonderful their husbands were doing, how much money they were making, or how wonderful everything was in their lives. She said she felt like she was in a competition with all these people, fighting to secure the status of success, power, money, or even love with their husbands. My mother really hated this 'bull shitting' but had to play the game in order to fit in with these other tai tai's, or otherwise face isolation. To her credit, she was not, in my eyes, one of the those *bak paw* police wives, who had nothing better to do than gossip and being nosy and at times causing harm and grief by spreading malicious rumours. Out of the pack, though, my mother did however make a couple of good friends. Neither of them were Cantonese—Sally and Mimi were both Shanghainese that had escaped to Hong Kong around the same time as my mother. They were keen mah-jong players, especially Mimi, and she was so addicted to gambling in the game that her husband, Charlie, had to bail her out of her debts! My mother felt so embarrassed for her, and quite clearly, Mimi had lost face with so many of her friends!

My early memories of my childhood were very happy ones. Apparently, I had a cute face, and everybody approved my baby face good looks! All of my mother's friends, who I called 'auntie', would always buy me sweets and take me out to yum cha(Cantonese tea). Of course, I was oblivious to the growing problems between my parents, yet I did get some idea from the armah, who always shuffled me away when their voices were raised. I think my father resented the fact that my mother being a 'tai tai' was not around to do the motherly things like cooking, cleaning, taking me to school, and going on day outs as a family. He was quite a traditional man in that sense and envisaged that my mother would do those maternal things that mothers do. With all respect and love to my mother, I cannot remember a time when she did any of those except when I was still in my pram! The armah was the face that I saw when I got up, to take me to kindergarten, to cook my meals, and serve it at dinner time. The bonding between my mother and both of us, my sister included, was not that close, unfortunately. She could not breastfeed us because her milk was unhealthy and gave us diarrhoea. It was as if she had done her duty of giving birth and reared us for a couple of years, and then she was free to pursue a life of a tai tai—her sense of independence, that she so zealously guarded, remained intact even into her later years.

My schooling for the first five years was in North Point at Quarry Bay School, an international school mainly for expatriates. I had such a great time there with other children that had a mixed background like mine—German-Chinese, Australian-Chinese, Portuguese-Chinese and other mixed Korean, Japanese, and Malaysian. Even at a tender age of six to nine years old, I felt totally normal and accepted by all the kids there that we were all mixed with east and west culture, and we could just be. There was no bullying, no teasing, no joking or mocking about our background, and the teachers there (mostly from the UK) were so supportive and understanding of all our backgrounds. All the teaching was in English and based on the school curriculum in the UK. There was hardly any Chinese spoken or contact with Chinese except for the cleaners, workmen, and canteen staff. It really was as if I was in school in the UK; we were cocooned into the British system of education and culture (just what my father wanted). I recalled a teacher called Mrs Wilson from Scotland who although she looked like a bit of a witch (with huge eyes and that famous prominent nose) and yet she was so patient and kind to me when I would struggle with some subjects like science. She never raised her voice at me or at other children, never saw her pull a child a side if they misbehaved, and certainly never hit anyone. All she had to do was to stare at you with those eyes! I remember I asked Mrs Wilson whether she liked Chinese people and Hong Kong itself and her gentle reply was, 'I love Chinese people, they are so polite and well behaved!' Having graduated from Quarry Bay, I regrettably never saw Mrs Wilson again. Clearly, both my parents saw that I was a happy child that enjoyed every moment of his school days, happy to be with so many kids from different backgrounds, and happy to be Peter Craggs—son to Inspector Harry Craggs. According to my mother, I was a model good child, always behaving and doing as I was told, hardly rebelling against my parents, and generally a quiet and shy individual. My sister, on the other hand, was like the 'black sheep of the family'—brash, cheeky, challenging, hyperactive, and generally annoying to both of them. She also developed a habit of telling lies and made up stories, a habit that was to continue into her adulthood and cause terrible problems for her! Unfortunately for her, my father called her that little 'b—h' of a daughter, and my mother used to hit her quite a lot with the bamboo end of the feather duster that was used to clean the apartment—Ouch!

My relationship with my father was very close—right up to his death. I liked almost everything he liked—football, goalkeeping, cycling, and going to the beach. Our favourite beach was Shek O, a more remote place than Repulse Bay and others, and it had excellent sand and great waves to surf. It was my father who always took my sister and I to the beach when he had time off (my mother didn't like the sun for fear of getting too dark in the sun!), and he took delight to see us appreciate the outdoor life in Hong Kong. He would not swim with us but just watched us from the restaurant, cooling off in the shade with his usual beer. Some of the happiest times of our lives were the days we went swimming at Shek O, and it was a great therapy for my father to have some breathing space from his mounting problems. Besides the beach, there was another favourite place where we all went together, the China Fleet Club. It was a huge social/restaurant/sports club for servicemen, and this was one of the rare opportunities where the expatriate husbands could bring along their Chinese wives and children and mingle and socialise with each other. It was one of the few occasions that my father did not mind my mother and the likes of me and my sister going to the club and using the facilities there while he was drinking the officer's mess. After all, the club was directly opposite Wan Chai Police Station, a convenient location for him and his colleagues to have cheap beers and a place to entertain the family at subsidised prices! I had very pleasant memories there because it reminded of the UK so much—really good Sunday roasts, regular football matches on TV, huge snooker tables that I used to mess around with, and my favourite place to have a hair cut! Today, the police station is still there, but, alas, the China Fleet Club was demolished long ago to make way for a gigantic commercial and retail outlet.

The moments of happiness in our family were few are far between, but when there were times and places we did come together well, they were really great! My happiness and apparent pleasant demeanour made me the favourite in the family in terms of attention from my parents, which then also extended to my mother's mah-jong friends. Whenever they came up to me, they would often pinch my cheeks because they thought I was cute—most annoying, I thought! However, as a blissfully naive youngster, my apparent reputation with everyone was that 'everybody liked Peter'. Yet I was totally unaware that simmering deep feelings of jealousy and resentment were developing in two of the closest people around me—my half-brother and sister. Sibling rivalry is a common occurrence in families, but I had never imagined that it (they) would come back and bite me with a vengeance! Out of the three children, I was fortunate to have experienced the happiest childhood, which I am extremely grateful for, and this has kept me going and has sustained me in my life so far. Child psychologists say that the first ten years of childhood are a time that really has the most significant imprint on a person's life and actually shapes the person for the rest of their lives—I would wholeheartedly agree with that!

Approaching Christmas 1965, it was time for my father's second 'on leave' trip back to the UK. I was six years old and my sister was four. This was the first time that I had real memories of the trip, and I could see the strain of my parents' marriage. Nana had insisted that we stay with her in Spohr Terrace South Shields, so that we could spend Christmas together as a family. My father's strained relationship with Nana created heated arguments with my mother, who, she thought, was wonderful to her on their first trip, but my father thought that spending six months in one household was just too much for him. His concerns turned out to be true. As kids, my sister and I were so excited because we were expecting to see snow the first time at Christmas, hearing and singing Christmas songs, presents from Father Christmas, and all the merriment of the season. Under the shimmering light of a real coal fire (the first time that I had ever seen one indoors) in Nana's front room, Christmas stockings were hanging waiting to be filled by Santa Claus with goodies. There is something about seeing a fireplace as it seems to enlighten and create an ambience of a communal spirit and peace within a confined space. I used to love using the fire poker and position the coal so that it could burn even brighter! Christmas cards adorned the shelf over the fire, and a real Christmas tree stood majestically glistening with the flashing lights and a tiny figure of sort stood at the top of tree—it was an angel. We were not disappointed. I know my mother was also quite excited because she wanted to see Nana again and spend some more time with her as she knew that her health was failing. Since we were going to be in South Shields for that time, I had to enrol for the local school across the bridge, and I had a brief but pleasant experience of a Geordie school system—Westoe Primary Schoo. Even in that brief schooling experience (three months) there I had picked up such a strong Geordie accent my friends could hardly understand me when I returned to Hong Kong! My father played along well for us children during the Christmas festivities, but once that was over, he started getting tense and irritated. The old issue of Audrey and this child was coming back to haunt him, and although I did not hear or see the discussions, I could sense that my mother was getting agitated. They thought (the Craggs's) that my mother's limited vocabulary of the English language would mask what was going on, but she saw the effect it was having on my father. She tried to comfort my father but to no avail. Auntie Mable and her husband Jimmy came round to visit, and they seemed to have added more fuel to the fire! He started to drink even more about the break and started going to the pub by himself. My father hired a car to drive us around Newcastle, and then on some evenings, he would stop at a pub, go in himself, and have a few beers while the three of us waited for him. It wasn't very pleasant for us waiting in the cold, but he did buy us fish n' chips and gave it to us in the car while we waited for him to finish his drinking session. Ever since that experience of eating in the car, my mother actually thought that, it was 'cosy and fun'!

I finally witnessed at first hand the tension between my father and Nana one evening. We had just finished dinner, which Nana had cooked. It was a cold evening, and she was putting more coal on the fire to keep us warm in her compact but damp home. My father was drinking already and had made a comment to Nana when suddenly she exploded with rage and took the fire poker and was about to hit my father on his head. Luckily, my mother intervened just in time to restrain Nana, and I recalled my mother saying 'please, Nana, don't, don't, don't'! I could see Nana shaking like a leaf, shouting some Scottish expression, cursing her son, which I could not understand. My mother ushered us into the bedroom to sleep, and once we got into bed, I heard the front door open and slam shut. The car engine fired up and revved with a sound of burning rubber. My father drove off for the night. Since that incident, my father decided it was time to leave and cut short his leave by about two months and fly us back to Hong Kong—he had had it with his mother. It was also the last we all saw Nana alive.

The times of the mid-1960s were exciting and interesting times when Hong Kong was heavily influenced by British and American culture. Television was now widespread throughout the wealthier population, and the main English channel: 'Radio Television Hong Kong' was broadcasting a mixture of British and American programmes. The Beatles were big, and I remember my father buying the album *Help* and that was the first time I saw what a thirty-three long-play record could do. I was absolutely amazed that a circular plastic disk could emit such great music! I liked using chopsticks (the armah taught me) to eat our Chinese meals, but I also found another ingenious use for them. I used them as drumsticks and would hit them on the sofa and play along with the Beatle songs—my favourite album was *Help*. According to my mother, she always heard me play and sing 'Dream, Dream, Dream' by Richard Chamberlain. I broke a lot of chopsticks, much to my mother's chagrin! In the apartments where we lived, there were other Chinese kids from the police force, and this is how I learnt Cantonese by playing with them after school. I had never received any formal learning in Cantonese, so I just followed what they said. I did learn some from my mother, but it was mostly to talk with the armah, ordering her to do things or telling her off! I also learnt how to play mah-jong by sitting beside her and watching her play when she invited her friends over for a game. I was very amenable to my mother's friends, as I volunteered to fill up cups of tea for all the aunties while they played. Mind you, I was well rewarded—either some extra pocket money or sweets! Although Hong Kong is a British colony, the television programmes, especially for children, were from America. My favourites were *Bewitched* and all the Warner Brothers' cartoons, others such as *Casper the Ghost, Felix the Cat*, and later there were *Hogan's Heroes McHale's Navy, I Dream of Jeannie,* and *The Monkees*. It was a strange combination of an upbringing for me—a British education but American entertainment and popular culture, which meant that I had an Anglo-American accent. My father was not impressed!

The summer of 1966 must have been the happiest times for most Englishmen—the England football team had won the World Cup for the first time on their home territory at Wembley Stadium—no wonder I didn't see much of my father! It was like England had conquered the world like the old empire days and the song 'Land of Hope and Glory' was played frequently on the TV and radio—a tune I hated to hear!

The more serious event of the times was the Vietnam War, which was raging on, and there was constant news of bombings and the horrendous casualties that resulted from the Americans' action. Every time I came home from school, to turn on the TV to watch my favourites, there were news bulletins about the latest military assault on the Vietnamese. One of my favourite toys was 'GI Joe Action Man', which portrayed the American soldier as the hero, almost like Superman. Whenever my father would hear the news about the Vietnam War on getting home, he would get so annoyed about the Americans and would curse them saying 'why don't they f—k off and keep their bloody noses out of other countries' affairs?' I did not understand the war. Across the border, something of a revolution was stirring up again—the Chinese Cultural Revolution. Mao, according to historians, was losing control of his country and wanted to reassert his power and influence on the people again. So he instigated a peasant revolution against the so-called bourgeois who were really the major industrialists and businessmen, alleging that they were a 'corrupt bourgeois ruling class that were exploiting the majority of the good honest people of the PRC'. Nearly everything was destroyed that represented Western bourgeoisies or middle-class status—from wealth, enterprise, history to culture, religion, and education. This was a potentially dangerous time for the tiny colony of Hong Kong, lying at the foot of the mighty motherland, as it represented all the Western decadence, which Mao and his Red Guards had sworn to destroy. It was reported many years later that the then paramount leader Deng Xiaoping stated that China, if it wanted to, could have marched across the border and take back Hong Kong from the British. Fortunately, it was not a priority for Mao then, and instead he focused on eliminating the so-called traitors and counter—revolutionary elements within the country itself. However, communist agitators had sparked riots in Hong Kong, alleging that workers at some factories had been sacked or their wages reduced dramatically by it owners—one of them being Li Ka-shing's flower business. With the possibility of destabilising the government and the society as a whole, the Hong Kong Police Force clamped down hard and fast on the rioters before they could gather any momentum. My mother recalls that my father was called to riot duty and would be away from home for some time. We were not allowed to go out in the evenings, something of a curfew, but schools were still open, and people continued with their everyday business. One of the more serious clashes between the left-wing supporters of Mao and the police occurred in 1967 at the border of Lok Ma Chau when five men of the Hong Kong police were shot dead by the Red Guards near the border crossing. This started to cause the government back in the UK some concern that this could get out of hand. For my father, fortunately, he was not ordered to go to the border but instead was trying to control a band of left-wing students that were rampaging offices and factories in Kowloon. According to my mother and some colleagues, my father had bravely held a police cordon on the front line to stop the students marching forward and was hit on the head by some object thrown by the rioters, with blood pouring out of his head. He told my mother that the local constables were *muk tau* (wooden-headed), meaning that they were basically useless and had no guts or initiative in dealing with that situation. Of course, he was seeing through his British eyes and did not understand that Chinese were not on the whole confrontational people, or that they believed confrontation can offer a solution. It was indicative that my father's impression of the Chinese, in general, was similar to that of the old colonialists of the earlier period of the British Empire, seeing and treating them in a rather patronising and dismissive way, labelling them as 'yellow', meaning that they lacked a certain amount of chivalry and courage. He was praised for his bravery, and of course, the expatriate community played on this to say 'how the British are courageously fighting and defending democracy and freedom for the Hong Kong people against the Red Communist Chinese'. I know my father was commended for his bravery, and another more senior officer turned out to be the hero of the police force—Peter Fitzroy Godber. Godber, originally from London, joined the force around the same time as my father but his route up the ranks of the force was much more progressive than my father's. It was reported that he had demonstrated superb leadership and man management in quelling a major riot in Hong Kong. From the media attention and eye-witness accounts of his command, the success of Godber's operation was later rewarded to him by a meteoric rise in the force from superintendent rank to that of a deputy district commander of Kowloon district. At least Commander Godber had done the expatriates a favour, by increasing the respect of the police officers from the local community in the work that they were doing in Hong Kong and defending their way of life from the mainland. For my father, there was no such luck in gaining promotion unfortunately, probably just a pat on his back on a job well done. Now that the police had reached new heights of respect and professionalism in handling the riots of 1967, the force had become more powerful, more influential, and with the Hong Kong economy expanding and money swishing around abundantly, more corrupt. On the one hand, the local Chinese were looking up to the police for how they defended them against the communists agitators, but at the same time, they saw these gweilo officers taking too many liberties and came over as rather arrogant and patronising. Corruption in the force was becoming endemic (apparently to make up for poor pay) and the governor was concerned that it was tarnishing its reputation. As far as my father was concerned, working in non-uniform Criminal Investigation Department (CID) had many privileges with the job. He would be able to enter any restaurant and bar and have free food and drink, free invitations to functions and parties, and generally have free access to a lot of services in the community. As a heavy drinker, and often drinking on duty, he was eventually found out by his boss and moved from CID—something that was quite common throughout the force, I am told. My mother told me that my father knew about Godber's reputation and that something big was going to happen to him and to the police force as a whole.

I was not disappointed in what I found from stories on the internet and the Hong Kong Police Force website about the endemic corruption problem. The then Commissioner of Police Charles Sutcliffe was determined to break the graft and widespread corruption, with Peter Godber one of the heroes of the 1967 riots singled out by Sutcliffe's investigations in 1973 as the leading officer involved in corruption and graft within the force.

As a result of this event, the Hong Kong Police lost all credibility with the local people, and the governor was compelled to set up the Independent Commission Against Corruption (ICAC) in 1976. It's purpose was to clear out, root, and branch all serving officers that had been in any way involved in bribes, favours, and unprofessional practices and conduct in the force. For Godber, it was a dramatic end to an illustrious career and also for those that were connected to him in some way. Alas, my father had not lived to see these developments and proceedings, and knowing his character, he would have voiced his strong views about what was going on. According to my mother, she told me that my father was keen to see that justice had been done and that this development would start the process to clean up the image of the police force. The positive side of this development was that the ICAC extended its powers to all government institutions and its workers and led a very successful campaign to clean up the image of Hong Kong as a safe and transparent hub for business, finance, and administration. It still is today doing the job of anti-corruption in Hong Kong successfully.

A pattern was developing in my father's police career. From the moment that I was born in 1959 up until his death in 1971, some thirteen years in the force, he had been moved from each division and area of his police work four times! Whether it was his request or that he was ordered to move is unclear, but the effect on my mother and us as children was quite destabilising. Just when we were getting used to living in an area and making new school friends and neighbours, we would have to move to a new area of police quarters, back and forth from Hong Kong side to Kowloon. By 1967, he had been an inspector now for fifteen years, and to see other colleagues getting to at least senior inspector or chief inspector must've demoralised him. His drinking now had made him into an alcoholic. He was approaching forty years old, with a solid twenty years of drinking behind him, which in turn affected his temperament, and in turn would cause more arguments and friction with my mother. My mother realised this was getting too serious to let carry on like this and tried to suggest him to see a doctor and psychiatrist to help him off his addiction. Her well-intentioned gesture however got her more into trouble with my father, and as a stubborn old Geordie copper, he would respond, 'Over my dead body.' My mother said he was so outraged that she knew better than him and to mention a psychiatrist and insinuate he had mental health problems was the ultimate insult. His retaliation to this was that he threatened my mother with words like 'fix her and send her back to China'.

This was serious stuff now going on between my parents, and as an eight-year-old, I could see that they were drifting apart. The sad thing about my father was that when he didn't drink, he was quite a gentleman and rather shy and retiring, according to my mother and even some her friends that met him. I vividly remember my father one day trying to unpeel an orange for me, and it was awful to see his hands shaking like someone who had Alzheimer's, turning the orange into one ball of mush! The shaking had gotten so bad that he virtually spilt a third of his cup of tea on to the saucer while he was drinking it. My mother genuinely felt sorry for him and tried to help, but as they say, 'alcoholics are always in denial of their problem'. From that moment, my mother was really concerned that the marriage was in serious jeopardy and feared for all of our futures—the three kids!

The Unwelcome Addition to the Family

In all the time I was growing up, my mother vaguely mentioned to me about this boy she had struggled to bring up and now wanted to introduce into the Craggs family. I remember, when I was around six years of age, this older boy would come and stay with us when his boarding school in Macao had holidays. He was rather strange looking, lean with curly light, almost ginger-coloured hair. His eyes and nose were more European looking than mine, and he always seemed to frown. To me, he did not seem to be a happy boy. He was nearly six years older than I was, so by the first time I met him, he was just into his teens. We seemed to play well together, and he would have some naughty ways that really made me laugh. One thing he showed me was how to make water bombs—filling small plastic bags with water and drop from the height of the apartments to the ground. They made a resounding splash and noise, which I enjoyed, but was actually very dangerous if they fell on someone! We used to enjoy flying kites the Chinese style. The kite would fly as far as the eye could see into the sky. He would cleverly manipulate the wheel of string to let his kite fly higher or manoeuvre it sideways. This young man knew of glass string which was sharpened with coarse sand, and this was used to manoeuvre the kite to get as close as possible and try to cut the string and bring the other person's kite down. There were other numerous games that he played, which showed that the boarding school he attended had taught him some very risky pastimes. I was so innocent compared to him! My sister, on the other hand, did not mix well with him or myself—she was always too challenging and rebellious for him to influence my sister. It was also the time she started telling little lies about everything and that would totally enrage both my parents, and hence she was beaten by my mother a lot more than I was! I was not close to my sister as youngsters; we always seemed to fight and argue, and she had her friends, while I had mine.

We had now moved to Blue Pool Road Police Quarters, which were up on a hill from the Happy Valley area. It was one of the happiest and the best places we stayed in, for a number of reasons. This is when I met Paul, who happened to live in Happy Valley on Wong Nai Chung Road, who later became my best friend. Happy valley is famous for the racecourse where thousands upon thousands of racing punters would make the place come alive on race days. We also had a great view from high up on the hill and could see the racecourse from a distance. When horse racing was not on, the green field was used for football, and I would go down there with my father to play football. I was already in the school football team (playing centre half) and my father was so proud of me that I was the only mixed kid in an all-white school team! Here we were, son and father, enjoying a sport that we both excelled in and a rare moment of enjoyment for my father. He didn't wear the appropriate kit when we were playing and still wearing his long work trousers and shoes, he decided that he would play as goalkeeper—what a coincidence. I recall that of all the people playing there on the Happy Valley football field, I hardly ever saw a father-son combination playing together. Most of them were kids like me or older semi-professionals on training. We did attract attention from the locals, where my father, with his stature and still wearing his office clothes, would be diving around the goalmouth from my shots—to my embarrassment at times! He seemed to put everything into it, his arms flailing about to parry shots and dive from corner to corner. He was coming alive, yelling and cursing himself at times with words like 'bloody hell, that's a good one, come on lad'! With sweat pouring from his head, his trousers covered in soil, and his shiny black office shoes blotted with grass and scuff marks, it was one of the few occasions that I saw my father have such a good time, sometimes bellowing in laughter and seeing a smile on his face that I had not seen before. He got so carried away that he beckoned more players on the field to take a shot at him—he did save well! At times, I was concerned for my father because diving around on that dry grass (which was bone dry) and having his rather corpulent beer belly hitting the ground might do some injury to him—I winced every time he fell heavily. The locals though were sniggering amongst themselves in this spectacle. It was a nostalgic time for my father and a treasured memory for me. On the days when he did have a weekend off, my father would drive my sister and me to Shek O beach and have a fantastic time of riding the waves. I could see why my father chose Hong Kong as it has great beaches just as South Shields has, and that in his youth, he would always go down there with his cousin Audrey.

The new brother had now been in boarding school for over ten years, and he had picked up a lot of bad behaviour. It's no surprise since he was starved of parental love, lacking any role models and all that family stability and support that is so vital to a balanced upbringing. My mother mentioned the fact that the cost of keeping him in boarding school was getting too much, and this was one of the main reasons why she tried to persuade my father to take him into the family. My father's inspector salary was just about able to maintain us four, but another mouth to feed and keeping an armah . . . ? I know my mother tried to keep paying his school fees from her own savings for as long as she could afford to do so, but by 1968, she had virtually used up all her money. After over ten years of school fee maintenance, my mother had to make a decision on how to assimilate this boy in the Craggs family. Back in the early days of their marriage, my father had insisted that this boy would not be part of their future and that was the condition that he would marry her. Then, some ten years later, she had hoped that everything would be stable—money, my father's job, home, marriage, children, etc. For some special reason that I have not been able to extrapolate from my mother right up to her last days, as to why she was determined to keep hanging on to this boy and integrate him into our family. Eventually, the issue had to be sorted out by my mother, which led to another heated confrontation between them. I recall my father shouting, 'That boy is trouble, and I will not accept him into my family!' My father knew by this time that his life was in crisis—the marriage was in trouble, his drinking was getting worse, he was loathing police work, and he was still getting pressure from Nana and Mable to deal with the Audrey issue. I recall that my mother did mention that one of the reasons that money was so tight (his drinks bill was mounting all the time at the officer's mess) was that my father was also sending money back to the UK to pay for some maintenance of this alleged child he had with Audrey. My mother admitted that she gave my father an ultimatum. 'You either adopt this boy as your son into the family, or I will leave you.' Her sense of timing could be devastating and obviously put my father on the back foot which he didn't like one bit! After a lot of wrangling and heart searching, my father decided to adopt the boy very reluctantly, and I can only guess that he did this because he still loved my mother enough and did not want us to be without a mother. In 1969, formalities were drawn up in the court, and the adoption papers were signed and confirmed—he was now officially the adopted son of Harry Craggs, a young teenager, aged fifteen years old. I do remember one late afternoon they both came back, and I saw my father having a sombre look on his face. He informed me, 'You and your sister now have a new brother!'

The new addition to our family looked glum, and retreated into the bedroom immediately, with his usual frown. I did have some understanding of what he meant but really didn't know about the adoption process. As far as I was concerned, it was good to have someone else to play with, and now my sister and I had an elder brother, who, we were told, would, from then on, stay and live with us on a permanent basis. It was a decision that my father bitterly regretted later, and in the last few years of my father's life, the tension between my mother and him over this young man grew worse and affected the whole family eventually. As far as my mother was concerned, she admitted that she was responsible for him and that sending him to boarding school (and not a very good one at that) totally ruined his childhood. She thought that integrating into the Craggs's would somehow make up for all the lost years from his childhood—and how wrong she was! He was damaged goods from the start.

Needless to say, one of the first signs that I saw of his dysfunction was that he never participated or went out with us kids for a day out. My father probably didn't want to invite him anyway, so he did his own thing. He had a better grasp of Cantonese than either of us, but his English was pretty poor. It's natural for teenagers to be rebellious, but his rebellion was too much for my father. He resented the fact that my father was laying the house rules and expected complete obedience as head of the household.

I remember quite clearly one weekend in our bedroom that we shared, he was confronting my father and shouting at him saying 'you are not my father'! Immediately my father gave him a good thumping, pinned him up against the wall, and said to him 'If you don't listen, I will throw you out on the street, and your mother can follow you as well!' Another incident that infuriated my father was the time he was stopped by the police on Waterloo Road for suspiciously carrying a large bag. When they searched inside, they found that he had stolen some ten to fifteen books from the local library. He was taken to the police station and held in custody until my father arrived to bail him out. It was a severe embarrassment to my father, especially as news travels fast within the force. My father said if it ever happened again, he would totally disown this adopted son and let him go. From that moment, their enforced father-son relationship went downhill pretty quickly. My mother was upset and could not control this teenager. I had begun to recognise that this half-brother had clearly been influenced by people involved in petty crime—a juvenile delinquent. The angst and resentment from both sides was now the major troubling issue between my parents. As he stayed with us longer, we no longer became so close half-brothers. I could see he was upsetting everyone. To me, he was now an intruder, a total stranger almost like an 'alien'. He was the major factor that finally ruined my parents' marriage.

The strain of this additional person raised the already heated arguments between my parents fourfold. Both of their temperaments were volatile and now we could clearly see that there were problems. To my father's credit, he made sure that we were in bed by 9.00 p.m. every night at the latest, so that we would not witness their arguments, a sort of damage limitation for us. We may not have seen so much, but my mother's voice carried and had a deafening presence about it. I was approaching my tenth birthday and by 1969, my parents had been married eleven years. According to my mother, my father had constantly mentioned that he was seriously considering quitting the force and said he was 'fed up and he wanted to pack it in'.

Nearly eighteen years in the force and still an inspector, and not much prospect of promotion or development for him, he thought. Not much good news for my father, but something very significant was about to occur to the police force as a whole. A major honour was bestowed to the police in 1969 by the Queen, when she gave her royal accent to the force, which would from then on be called the 'Royal Hong Kong Police Force'. This was given in recognition of its professionalism and its well-managed strategy in dealing with the 1967 left-wing riots. With such recognition and elevated status, it was the first of its kind in the colonial forces in Asia, and it was an extremely proud moment for the Hong Kong Police. There was even a book published about the force called *Asia's Finest* and written by a well-known local expat journalist Kevin Sinclair, which boosted its image to an international audience. I remember my mother saying to me that she was so proud that my father was working in an organisation that had royal approval—a rare moment when I saw a glint of emotion in her eyes and a sense of pride in my father. On a more personal level, my father was presented with a cup (which I still proudly keep as well as his cup trophies from his football achievements) from his colleagues at Western Police station officer's mess in 1969 for his services to the force. Even this could not tempt him to think that he could serve another ten years or more and retire with a generous fat pension. Since its royal accent, there were more new recruits of junior expat inspectors to join the force, especially now with its royal title, and the perks were even better than my father's generation. For my father however, he probably felt threatened by these young blood officers snapping at his heals. He was an old-hat and one with a problem!

The Last Trip Back to the UK

Approaching Christmas 1969, we were to embark on another leave break and the last one for my father and as it turned out the last for the Craggs family. It was for me the most memorable one of all the trips to the UK and one that I was mature enough to see as to how my parents' marriage was falling apart. On the positive side, I was so excited to go there again, see Nana and Auntie Mable, and taste the Northern fish and chips! However, my mother warned me that we might not stay with Nana this time after the last visit in 1965. This time I understood the circumstances. This visit would be significantly different this time in one aspect—my brother would be joining us. Clearly, my parents' relationship was deteriorating rapidly, and the friction between my father and my brother was blatantly obvious. They were hardly on speaking terms now, and my mother had to be present always whenever they were in the room together. It was awful! Still with all that going on, our trip was also going to be very different—we would travel by boat and cruise all the way to Europe, fully paid for, of course! My sister and I were ecstatic as the only boat we'd really been on before was the Star Ferry crossing the harbour. We were told that the journey would take four to six weeks, and we would see many countries on the way and meet lots of people on the boat. We were not disappointed! Again, the timing was planned for us to reach there just before Christmas so as to have some family gathering, and that meant we left around late November 1969. I asked my father whether we could play football on the boat—he chuckled and gave me a hug. My mother however was a little apprehensive because she was prone to seasickness, and the thought of spending so much time out to sea—not a holiday in her eyes. I think my father deliberately planned to go by sea because it was a good way to pass the time instead of a boring journey of a sixteen-hour flight cooped up in the plane. Also later I found out that he didn't want to spend all his leave time in the UK. On the whole, everybody was looking forward to the trip after my father had mentioned how many countries we would visit and see other countries' cultures. Only one person was miserable: my brother—my mother said he didn't even want to go and preferred to stay in Hong Kong with his friends. My father had said, 'That ungrateful miserable so and so, leave him here!' My mother had somehow persuaded my father to include him.

The name of the cruise liner was the *Asia*, part of the P&O shipping company. Her sister ship was the *Oriana*, and they were huge ships that did the trip from Hong Kong to Europe on a regular basis. I remember the ship docking at Ocean Terminal (which is still used today), and this gigantic mass of white metal docked elegantly alongside the quay. I tried to count all the windows it had on it, but I gave up! On the day we boarded, there were huge crowds gathered at the terminal waving goodbye to their relatives and friends, most of them happy and laughing and some in tears. We as a family were quite low-key, with one of my father's colleagues seeing him off, and a couple of my school friends having come to wave goodbye. They really wanted to come with me, and they were sad to see me go, with one friend, Robert saying, 'If you don't come back, I'll take your football team place!' There was no way I was going to let that happen!

Fortunately, for Hong Kong, the water in the harbour is deep and can accommodate big ships and liners. So whenever a liner was to dock at Ocean Terminal, it was a great attraction for tourists and locals to see. As we finally disembarked from Ocean Terminal with the liner reversing ever so slowly (it had to avoid the multitude of junks, sampans, and the Star Ferry scurrying across) I was holding my father's hand and noticed he looked rather emotional. I said to him, 'Why do you look so sad, Dad?' He looked ahead for the moment, seeming to search for an answer, and then pulled me aside and replied, 'It's all right, lad. I don't know how many trips we can have like this.' It was an ominous observation. We all continued waving goodbye until the actual people just became specs of colour from a distance. The liner chugged cautiously by HMS Tamar with a sudden sounding of the horn from the liner, which made me jump. The view was great: the mountains of Hong Kong side overshadowing the offices of Central with the sun's reflection almost glistening on the water's surface and seeing the trail of bubble water churned out from the propellers of the ship's engines. My father was still gazing ahead, lost in some private thought, and his hand firmly gripping mine. My mother and sister were standing somewhere else. The half-brother was nowhere to be seen.

The *Asia* was scheduled to stop at nine seaports in nine countries as far as I can remember. The stops were: Hong Kong to Singapore, to Kuala Lumpur, then on to Madras, and to Bombay, India. The journey would have been shorter if we were able to go through the Suez Canal, but this was closed due to the 1967 war between Israel and Egypt. So it was re-routed around Africa and would take us to Mombassa in Kenya and then right down to Durban and Cape Town, South Africa. Then we would sail up to West Africa to stop at Lagos, Nigeria, then on to Algiers, and then to enter the Mediterranean Sea and dock at Barcelona, with the final stop in Trieste, Italy. It was a good geography lesson for me, and it was also an opportunity to collect more stamps from these countries as I was building my stamp collection. Once we had lost sight of Hong Kong and some of the islands, we went inside the ship where a smartly dressed steward in all white uniform greeted us in strange English accent—he was Italian. He allocated our cabins to us, and we three children were given bunk beds next door to our parents. My father was clearly delighted that everything was so organised and that it was a trip he was really looking forward to—and so was I!

Life on the *Asia* for my parents was one of familiarisation and getting used to the constant rolling from the waves of the sea. My father would wake early in the morning and head straight to the top deck to get some fresh sea air. He always liked the sea as it reminded him of his happier youth days in South Shields beach back home. My mother, however, usually slept in late, which annoyed my father, probably because she was not used to the constant rolling of the ship. She nearly always missed breakfast, and sometimes she would have the steward bring it to their room and leave it outside their cabin for her to collect—not very often. It was clear to me that my father wanted to experience everything that the cruise trip had to offer, going to all decks, seeing how the ship operated, talking to some chief stewards, and of course find out where all the bars were. Most mornings, we would head down to the breakfast before eight (without our mother) and have all goodies, different kinds of cereals, cakes, breads, and Italian ice cream! I noticed that the waiting staff were quite nimble on their feet, especially when the ship would suddenly lurch to the side and hold on to the trays barely spilling anything. I was amazed to see that teapots, cups, and saucers did not slide on the silver trays until one day I asked how they did that. The waiter showed me that there was a wet napkin placed underneath the plates and saucers on each tray that would almost glue them to the tray. I asked my father, 'Would it stick if I held it upside down?' He chuckled.

There was a lot to do for both adults and children for most of the day. There were swimming pools on each deck, volleyball, deck bowls, table tennis, and a theatre showing some new films. As a rather shy and retiring youngster, I surprised myself in how many friends I made from so many different backgrounds. Since we were going to so many countries, there were people from those countries that would disembark as soon as we arrived at each port.

One of the most interesting and challenging places was our two-day stopover visit to Bombay. It was an important stopover because the liner had to stock up for provisions and food and a general maintenance check before the next stop to Africa. My father was not that keen in meeting Indians and swore to my mother that he would not be going ashore. It was the first time I saw such poverty even from on board the liner, seeing in the distance the shanty buildings, primitive transport, and the shabby-looking people in their attire. What really struck me was the smell of the harbour water and the general air quality, and when I looked down at the quayside, I could see why! As soon as we docked, the local Indians rushed on board like excited children, eyes wide and smiling with glee as if they had seen a UFO. My mother was keener to find out about Bombay, but without my father going, she remained on the boat. Instead, one very interesting merchant that my mother got help from was a local chiropodist who offered to remove all her corns and hard skin from her feet (from all those years of wearing high-heeled shoes). My mother was always complaining about her feet and gave this chiropodist a chance to treat them. I saw him scraping, washing, and using strange instruments on her feet. The most gruesome thing he did was that he made an incision on each of my mother's corns right on the ball of her foot and then put a funnel on it as if it was being used to suck out something. After about fifteen minutes, he removed the funnels and revealed what looked like some nerve endings in blood, and he then exclaimed, 'See all mother, father, and children roots are out now!' My mother was hysterical with laughter and clearly delighted—I think that was the highlight of the trip for my mother!

By the second week on the liner, we were sailing towards the continent of Africa, and my father mentioned that it was a blessing in disguise that the Suez Canal was closed. It meant for all of us a longer journey on the boat and for my father more time to enjoy drinking from bar to bar, chatting and meeting people, and some romancing time with my mother. She enjoyed the evening entertainment where there were dances and live bands, and she told me that my father even enjoyed dancing with her on the floor. I thought that maybe they could repair some of the damage in their relationship and asked my mother, 'Is Dad being kind and friendly to you?'

She hesitated for a moment and then a rather annoyed expression came across her face as she replied, 'Yes, your father is a gentleman, but when he drinks too much, he is just not pleasant!' I knew what she meant.

The other significant part of the trip was the stop in South Africa. My father mentioned that he had a good friend called Jack and that he was looking forward to meet him. When we arrived at Cape Town, I was totally awestruck by the famous Table Mountain that seemed to dominate the skyline. It seemed so flat that I thought you could land a plane on it! We were scheduled to stop for three days and go ashore and join a tour of the city. It was my first experience of seeing so many black African people who seemed to be so relaxed and moping about the street without a care in the world. When we had entered a restaurant to eat, there was a sign saying 'Whites only Restaurant', and I could not understand what that meant. My father replied, 'Those blacks are not allowed to eat with us because they are backward and behave like animals!'

Neither of my parents was very keen on dark-skinned people. I was too young to argue with his view. When we strolled down the street, I could see that the local black population was separated from the whites by different streets and that police patrolling the streets would watch where the black were walking to. Apartheid was well and truly alive. Towards the last day of our stopover in Cape Town, mum told us that Dad was seriously thinking of living in South Africa with Cape Town in particular because of its more British connections rather than Afrikaans in other parts of country. To me, it seemed a good choice because the weather was similar to Hong Kong, and Cape Town had great beaches and plenty of outdoor life. As we waved goodbye to Cape Town, I noticed that my father was in a better mood than usual—he seemed to have found a way out of Hong Kong and create another future for himself and had made plans to quit the police force.

The weather was great all around the trip to Africa. Virtually every day was sunny, and hundreds of deckchairs were always being used by people. Lots of sport activities were happening, and there was a table tennis competition being organised by the crew for passengers to compete in. My father was an enthusiastic player but rather too big and bulky to look very elegant playing the game, and my brother also entered himself into the competition. I had seen him play, and he played like a local Chinese—a penholder grip and very aggressive in his shots. It just so happened that in the second or third round my father was drawn to play him. I was excited for the match, father and son against each other, but this is where I saw his resentment towards my father. On every point he won, he really jumped for joy, yelling something in Cantonese, which I could not understand and revelling in the thrashing of my father. It was as if he wanted to humiliate my father in front of people—and he did by winning easily. When the game ended, my father's expression said it all, and he extended his hand to congratulate him—he refused the handshake. I could see him sniggering away as he walked back to his cabin, and after that event, he was not invited to join us on any activity for the rest of the cruise. Other than that unpleasant encounter with his adopted son, I could see that my father was having a good time, and whenever he did, he whistled—alas not that often in Hong Kong! For my mother, however, the seasickness was annoying her, and she found it difficult to sleep at night. He tried to cheer her up and bring her food personally to the cabin, and on one occasion, I saw him embrace her and give her a very intimate kiss—a rare sight indeed! I was hopeful that maybe they could make up and be nice to each other, and at times like these, they seemed so much a couple, but my mother would suddenly switch her mood and shrug him off with a comment like 'Oh, you just want to go back to the bottle after you do this to me!' His reaction would be one of exasperation.

Our ship was now on the last part of the journey, heading towards the Mediterranean via one more African port—Lagos Nigeria. It was the worst stop of the whole journey. I thought Bombay was bad and smelly, but Lagos took the prize. It had everything that Bombay had, but the local

Nigerians behaved like a mob in their shouting, screaming, loud, and obtrusive behaviour. My father was enraged, and I could see in his red-faced complexion as to how annoyed he would get, as he would mumble in his Geordie accent. 'You kids are not to go out playing like before until we leave this bloody place, understood?' I meekly obeyed as I normally did, but my sister was a little more challenging and kept asking our mother why, why, why . . . ? We did venture out and still play and swim, but my father was close by and always looking over his shoulder. I couldn't understand my father's anger towards these people as especially he was considering moving to South Africa where there were plenty of them. But with Apartheid, he/we would be living under segregation laws so that took care of the problem for him. A relief to almost everyone was when we left Lagos after three days, but we took on-board more passengers from Nigeria that changed the complexion of the journey. As far as I was concerned as a kid, they seemed ebullient, fun loving and always had a smile on their face. I was impressed by the women's dresses with multicoloured designs that wrapped their shapely figures in an elegant and tidy way. Added to this was their headdress, which matched the design of the dress, carefully groomed and shaped to add a height to their womanly bodies—impressive! Music was always on their lips as they would be singing their traditional songs, and some had actually brought their drums and instruments and played on the decks morning, afternoon, and night. They were a highly active people, always moving, and they had rhythm that I had never seen before. As far as I could gather from the other white passengers on board, they seemed to enjoy their company and were mostly welcomed. From a rather cocooned colonial upbringing in a Chinese city like Hong Kong, I had received an African education for the first time in my life—and it was pleasant!

On to the tip of North Africa and Algiers for a whistle-stop visit, we were now in Europe and the Mediterranean Sea. As we left Algiers, my father said with a huge sigh, 'Not long to go, lad, only Spain and then our last stop Italy.' I was sad too, for after about five weeks of sun, sea, fun, and games, it was coming to a rapid end. Barcelona was a pleasant experience and something more familiar to my father and mother. It was a short stay, as I recall, and all we did was go to the main shopping area and buy some souvenirs. My father was not keen on Spanish bars as they served tapas and lots of wine—neither of which he liked. For my mother, she was delighted to do some good shopping like buy some shoes and handbags and wear some the traditional Basque costumes. I remember that the women in Barcelona always had bright red lipstick to be contrasted by their jet-black hair, and my mother tried to copy this fashion. It appealed to my father, and I remember my father hurried us to bed so he could have some intimate time with her! The last leg of the trip was the shortest from Barcelona to the Italian port of Trieste, and the ship captain arranged for a big farewell party for all the passengers to celebrate the end of the journey. It was a day that was both happy and sad as people had made lifelong friendships and dare I say it some men and women had become a couple. For my parents, my father would miss the acquaintances he had made of the ship, especially with the bar staff and a couple of chief stewards, and for my mother, I think, she was relieved that all the rocking and rolling was soon coming to an end. Once we arrived at Trieste, my father had arranged for us to visit Venice as a treat for us and savour the gondola and the ancient city. It was a wonderful visit, and being rowed in the gondola through the narrow canal was such fun. It was also fun seeing some old buildings just above sea level. My father tried to serenade my mother and sing a song (which I can't remember) while we were navigating the canals on the gondola, and he had my mother hysterical (he was not singer). She remarked 'saw gweilo!', which meant you silly white man. We spent about three days in Venice, and when that came to an end, we were to cross Europe by train to finally arrive Calais and then cross the channel to the UK.

Once we arrived at Calais, my father announced that we would not be going to see Nana in South Shields—to everyone's disappointment. I remember my mother tried to persuade him to change his mind or at least let us go and visit her, but when he made his decision, it was final. We were all pretty tired by the time we arrived at Dover, and as my father was about to pick up a hired car, he announced to us that we were going to stay in Southampton and meet cousin Auntie Shirley—Auntie Shirley? My father had made not one mention to us before about her, and my mother too had no idea that he had a cousin living in Southampton. It was miles away from Geordie land and right down on the South Coast of England. It is however a major port for the navy and for commercial seagoing vessels and container port. Once we arrived, we were greeted by Aunt Shirley in a wheelchair and her husband, Dave. From what I could gather from my mother, Aunt Shirley was the daughter of my granddad's brother, which I suppose made us third cousins. She was about the same age as my father but looked bloated and had this unhealthy pink complexion on her face. She spoke with a Geordie accent and had married Dave, who was a local to Southampton—hence Southampton. We stayed at their compact council house for few weeks until we found a house that we could rent and eventually found one, to my mother's relief.

As I recall, the whole stay in Southampton was largely an unpleasant one for all us. My brief recollection and the encounter with Aunt Shirley was that she was a miserable woman who had become wheelchair bound due to her drinking addiction (again) and who treated her husband, Dave, like a slave. I always smelt the breath of alcohol on her, even during the daytime, and each time she met my dad, they would have a serious debate about something. That something, according to my mother, was that my father was letting the side down—the Craggs's. He was being ridiculed for not visiting Nana, especially when her health was failing and for not seeing his sister, Mable. The issue of Audrey was also mentioned and the events around her, and this haunting was to come full circle again. To my father, this was not a relaxing break (thank God for the cruise he must've thought), and to face these people and hear the same old issues again was too much for him. My mother said that after the cruise he promised her that he would go 'cold turkey' with alcohol and kick the habit—a gesture that really touched her heart. He did try to go without a drink for a couple of weeks, my mother said, but when she saw him sweating profusely and shaking as if he was in excruciating pain, she could not bear the sight of him suffering like that.

One day when my sister and I were playing in the green house in the back garden (we had never been in a green house before, and it was a delightful place for us to play) two adults suddenly appeared in the back garden. I said to the lady, 'I think I know who you are because I have seen a picture of you?' She smiled and said, 'And who do you think I am, young man?' It was Auntie Mable and Uncle Jimmy. They had come all the way down from Newcastle, probably from Aunt Shirley letting them know that my father had arrived back in the UK. From the moment they visited and finally caught up with my father, he hit the bottle. My mother was furious, and I heard her say to my father 'let's get out of here as soon as we can.'

I think he agreed, and he was making plans to end the rental agreement early for the house that we were staying in. Aunt Mable and Jimmy didn't stay long, but their presence was enough to disturb my father's peace of mind and his attempt to get off alcohol for good. All I could see that from my father's face (in stark contrast to the cruise experience) was his frown and his mumbling of 'bloody hell' whenever Mable was mentioned. He was informed that Nana was in poor health and probably didn't have much time—that upset him as well. As much as my mother tried to give him support in these circumstances, it led to more heated arguments between them, and that honeymoon period aboard the *Asia* was now well and truly gone.

Besides the adult issues that were going on, there were only a couple of significant memories for me on this trip. One was seeing the live broadcast of the American astronaut Neil Armstrong's landing on the moon, with the infamous phrase 'that's one small step for man, one giant leap for mankind.' The other being a TV programme called *Cat Weasel*, which I watched religiously.

I believe my father had signed a rental agreement for four months for the house, but with everyone so miserable and stressed, he decided to terminate after only two months. He had decided to cut short his leave (which was still three months to go) and we would all leave Southampton and UK early and fly back to Hong Kong. None of those relatives saw us off, and we—the kids—didn't have the chance even to talk to Nana on the telephone. In all this time, my brother just hid himself in his room, totally alienated from the rest of us. My father would often say he was 'fed up', and so was I—I was missing my school friends and missing Hong Kong.

My father in the army.

Early days on South Shield beach (on right)

In the school football team (second row, second from left)

Nana in South Shields

On the winning team, Northern Police Cup (in the middle between the men in coats)

On the winning team, HK Police Force (back row last on right)

His early drinking days in HK (right)

Our second trip back to South Shields with friends

Mother, sister and myself on our travels

Mother, half-brother and myself (me on left)

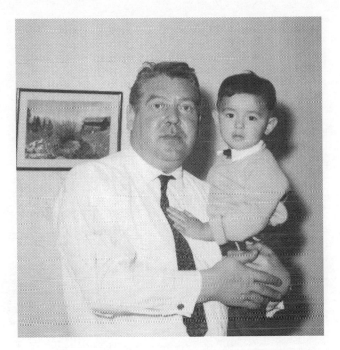

Fellow Geordie friend of my father, Uncle Ted and myself

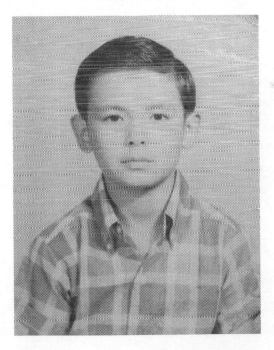

Just before I left Hong Kong for the UK

Our proud house in Mitcham

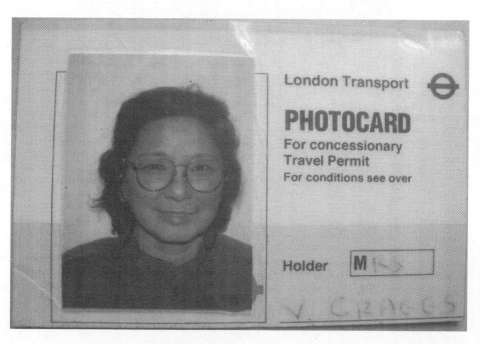

My mother living the London life

Mother, friends and myself in Cyprus

Happier times with my mother's mainland relatives

My mother, a true survivor and myself in China

Last picture of my father and on his
grave in Happy Valley cemetery

Near her end, my mother in the nursing home in the UK

The Last Move

We were all relieved to have arrived back home, and this time when I spoke with my friends, I didn't have a Geordie accent! It was now early 1970, and we had only spent three months away out of six from my father's last leave entitlement. We did not return to the quarters in Blue Pool Road (sadly) and instead we had to stay in the Miramar Hotel in Kowloon, because we were waiting to be housed in new police quarters in Kowloon. Again, my father had been moved to Kowloon Side and would now be working as the senior police prosecutor at South Kowloon Court. It was the last posting of his career and of his life. These moves did not do us any favours as children, because it was unsettling in terms of schooling and having to readjust to a new neighbourhood. My sister and I were upset because Happy Valley was such a great location and had all the facilities we wanted to use, and being on the island, it was an easy access to the beach, especially Shek O—Hong Kong Island has all the best beaches. I was particularly upset because my best friend, Paul, would not be close by, and I was now living on the other side of the harbour—it seemed a long, long away. I think my father wasn't too happy about the move either because he had most of his friends on Hong Kong Island, and there was a greater population of gweilos there—he used the phrase 'fed up' again. He also told me that he would miss playing football with me in Happy Valley. At first, living at the Miramar Hotel was fun and convenient as everything was prepared for us, and the breakfasts were scrumptious! However, the novelty wore off after a month, and I was moaning to my mum about missing a playground to play in and not being able to see my friends after school. My parents both understood, and I could see my father making calls to his boss on a regular basis to find out when we could finally settle into our new home. After nearly two months, my father was given the quarters, and we could move at last—they were called Ho Man Tin Mansions on Ho Man Tin Hill Road. It was a convenient location for my father to get to South Kowloon Court as Ho Man Tin was on a hill, and we could see the courthouse from the apartment block. It also overlooked Wylie Road where the famous Wai Yan College is based, and Waterloo Road and Nathan Road were just ten minutes walk down the hill. This final move turned out to be the unhappiest, most troubling, and causing the utmost marital strife between my parents.

It was obvious to all of us that my father was very unhappy about his work, his married life, and, sad to say, his role as the head of the family. Certainly, the last trip back to the UK didn't help and those family members were still on his back. Once we had moved to Ho Man Tin, it was decided that we did not need an armah—or probably that we could not afford one any more. My father was drinking even more since our return, and his frustration and resentment were being passed on to my mother. She was not going to tolerate it any more. My mother was now seriously considering a separation from my father and sought legal advice from a well-known family solicitor Helen A Lo. Apparently, it was not the first time that my mother had spoken with Helen Lo but was then advised by Ms Lo to hang on and see if he would change. Helen Lo suggested to my mother that counselling and marriage guidance services might help both of them. Again, my father felt insulted and threatened my mother that he would 'fix her and send her back'. According to my mother, the stress and the increased arguments between them led her to take tranquillisers to help her to sleep, and even having the odd gin or whisky as well. This was getting very serious, and now they were not even sleeping together in the same bedroom. Instead, I was to share the bed with my father, and my mother went to sleep with my sister. My brother had his own room. I noticed that my father would come home later than before and hardly ever have dinner with us. When he arrived home, the smell of alcohol permeated the whole living room, and his mood would be foul at times. Once the clock hit nine o'clock, it was bedtime for us—no ifs or buts! The reason my father enforced this so rigorously was he wanted to shield us from the heated exchanges he had with my mother. We were lucky that we didn't see the confrontation, but we did certainly hear it, but after ten minutes of hearing their voices, I would trail off into my dream. I remember that on some occasions my father would accidentally wake me when he got into bed, and I would say to him 'don't argue with Mum, Dad'. He would whisper to me and say 'go to sleep, lad, it's OK', and then give me a hug with the strong smell of alcohol on his breath.

I had started school at Kowloon Junior, which was one of the best international schools in the area. It was just as mixed as Quarry Bay, with kids from various parts of the world, but still the majority were British expatriates. What helped me to integrate better into the school was that they spotted that I was good at football, and within the first month, I made it into the first team, playing the position of centre half—again I was the only Anglo-Chinese in the team. My dad was proud of me! The one noticeable difference about living in Kowloon Side, and being not that far from Mong Kok and Tsim Sha Tsui, was that we were predominantly living in a high-density local Chinese area and at the doorstep of the Nathan Road, with all the shopping frenzy that accompanied it—it is a unique place. For my mother, she was glad to be back in Kowloon, as most of her friends lived on the mainland. Her main two friends, Sally and Mimi, lived in Kowloon district (Lai Chi Kok and Austin Road), and they would often come over to play mah-jong and vice versa, and this is how we as kids got to know each other's family. There was another friend Sissy, who was married to Ted, who was also a Geordie ex-police officer from North Shields whom we came to know well, and we were able to build a new neighbourhood network of friends. From my experience of being Anglo-Chinese and meeting these kids of a mixed background (especially from police force backgrounds), I really did not get along very well with them. I don't know what it was then, but today I understand it to be lack of identity or a sort of inferiority complex that put a barrier between us. I thought they were weird, and they probably thought that of me as well! Most of my friends then were like Paul, who was of Greek/Irish/Portuguese mix, or Robert of Anglo-Indian, and a few others of Korean, Japanese, and Malaysian backgrounds. My impression was that the Anglo-Chinese wanted only to identify with British and only that, hardly integrating with local community in which they lived. Even today, when I travel back to Hong Kong, this attitude remains the same, and it especially applies to girls/women who always seem to choose a gweilo as a boyfriend or a husband. Yes, probably I'm weirder than them!

This last posting for my father had him saying to my mother, 'I've had enough of this job, Hong Kong, and this life. I am going to pack it in!' He already had his good friend, Jack, in Cape Town whom he had met on our cruise, who may help him settle there and find work. There was also the option of Australia (the 'Ten Pound Pom' emigration programme), where there were some opportunities for my father to rebuild a life there and for bringing us along as well. He mentioned to my mother that he would do a complete change in his work—driving buses and coaches and even working as a milkman! He always enjoyed driving, and this influence probably came from his days in the army as a truck driver when serving in the Palestine War. It was significant that he not once considered going back to the old country and having to face those people. There seemed to be a pattern where a large majority of expats who retired early (forty-five plus) did not want to go back to the UK for various reasons. They thought that the old country was too highly taxed, had bad weather and poor prospects, and having to start all over again at a lower level was not acceptable to them. My mother said that that was when she wanted to seek a divorce from him. Again, she turned to Helen Lo for marital advice and wanted to seek a divorce based on physical and emotional abuse, but the response from Helen was not that encouraging. She was told that there was not enough evidence of physical violence having been inflicted by my father upon her to have a strong case in the divorce law courts and win custody of the children. The fact that my mother was from China was also a significant disadvantage to her in the British courts, and they would see her status in an unfavourable way. I was astounded to find out years later that my father had not applied for a British passport for my mother, and he had made no effort to get her one. All she had was residency under the British Nationality Act by the fact that she married a British subject. I thought that was cruel of my father, but I know he had his reasons and justification for not having gone through with this important application for my mother. We all finally got our passports because of the help from Uncle Hugh (Aunt Sally's husband), who did the paperwork for us after my father died.

So, for my mother, I can understand her distress and desperation. She was certainly not young any more in her late forties with no real work skills. She had limited ability in English, and of course had us three children to raise. She told Helen that he was not capable of being a responsible father and that he was irresponsible with money (he had run up huge drinking debts in the police messes, which my mother had to pay off for him). With his alcoholism and temperamental nature, she would have a better chance of looking after the children—so she thought. Helen just told my mother that she could divorce my father quite easily but to have custody of us was another matter. My father had many a times, during their intense arguments, said, 'You can bugger off, but leave the kids to me.' Some of her friends (Auntie Khan, Ah Law) had warned my mother years ago that Harry had a serious drinking problem, and staying with him would be difficult and traumatic—they were right to a certain extent. Where could my mother turn to? At times before I went to bed, I would try to comfort my mother and say, 'Mum, I hope Dad comes home in a better mood and not be too drunk', and I could see the tears welling up her eyes.

By the summer of 1970, we were more settled as kids in the Ho Man Tin area. What was good for the all children in the blocks of flats was that we had a good-sized playground where we played football and a huge (by Hong Kong standards) car park where we used to ride bicycles and run around. This is where I learnt to improve my Cantonese and actually felt for the first time that I could relate and play with Hong Kong people. The Ho family lived opposite us. The head of the family was a chief inspector in the force, who my father knew about, but he kept his distance from Chinese officers in general. However, I really made good friends with his three sons, all of whom were as fanatical about football as I was. We would head straight down to the playground after school had finished and play until up to dinner time when my mother, much to her annoyance, had to come down and drag me home to do some homework. Sometimes I would be invited back to the Hos for a typical Cantonese dinner, usually a lot of soup, rice, fish, and Chinese egg tarts (*dan tart*). In hindsight, I treasured the time we had in Ho Man Tin (only eighteen months in total) because in that short space of time I truly felt integrated into the Hong Kong society. I saw at first hand how cultured and well mannered they were and seemed to be able to combine the best of the east and west together. The Hos made it a rule that dinner would be served at 7.00 p.m., six days out of seven (Sunday was a day for dim sum or evening dinner in the city), and that all the family had dinner together unless the father was on shift duty. Near their typical Chinese round dinner table, made of rosewood, were the statues what looked like three elderly men, all with different costumes and expressions but look serene and wise. Incense would be burnt, and there would be a bowl of fruit as an offering to the statues. I asked Ah Luen what was all this about, expressing my ignorance about their culture, and he responded by saying that three wise men blessed their home, food, family, and give protection from evil spirits. I immediately thought as to why couldn't we have these wise men in our family and help the problems between my parents. On the other hand, the Hos had all the modern living standards that my Western friends had, watched some English programmes, studied in both English and Chinese, and had holidays in Europe and North America. Having dinner at the Hos made me proficient in the use of chopsticks! I lost touch with the Hos after we left Ho Man Tin, and I later found out that all three of their sons had been sent to Canada to further their studies where they probably made a new life for themselves.

One of the other big sporting occasions left for my father to witness was the 1970 World Cup held in Mexico. Since England were the reigning world champions, my father was particularly keen to see his home country do well, and I clearly remember that most of the Hong Kong people wanted England to do well. At my school, Kowloon Junior, there were Union Jack flags and posters hung on the school gates with the slogan 'Come on England!' I could sense that my dad's spirit had lifted a bit, and he was pleasantly distracted by the games for the next few weeks. As much as he disliked the old country like many of his compatriots, in his heart he would always support England in football. I recall that on days of the crucial England game against his favourites, Brazil, my father would take the whole day off to watch it live at home with his usual San Miguel by his side.

I once said to my father, 'Dad, it's good to see you so happy and not moan so much about everything.' He gave me a pat on the head, marched to the sofa, and watched the game as if he was hypnotised.

During the game, he would curse the usual Geordie slang and express his exasperation, and I would copy him—like father, like son I suppose. His enthusiasm and excitement reminded of the times we played football together in Happy Valley as if he was reliving his youth and happier days. England lost 1-0. After that defeat, they made it through to the quarter-finals but were eventually knocked out by West Germany, who then made it to the final. West Germany faced Brazil in the final, where Brazil won and became the World Champions for the third time! My father would say in his own words that 'genius Pele lad was magic'. It was the best time I spent with my father in Ho Man Tin.

After a fun-packed summer, I was to start the new school term at King George V secondary school. It was the natural progression from Kowloon Junior to KGV, and their buildings were actually right next door to each other. My mother once remarked that seeing us grow up so quickly reminded her of how short life can be. She was not prone to be reflective or philosophical about life, but with the marriage crumbling and her husband being a severe disappointment, she was feeling quite depressed. She too was drinking more but not to the level of my father and still taking those pills, as she says, 'to calm me down and not be upset by your father'. Added to this, she told me years later at that time she was going through menopausal changes, which made her feel highly sensitive, short-tempered and volatile. What a time to have this, I thought! It's no wonder that their arguments got worse. I can categorically say that out of all the places I had been brought up and lived in, Ho Man Tin's atmosphere had the utmost tension and stress for all of us. Again, I was to discover years later, the land that Ho Man Tin flats were built on covered a mass burial site of local Chinese that were killed by the Japanese army when they occupied the territory during WWII. Knowing how superstitious Hong Kongers are about such events, they told me that the area was cursed with the tormented spirits of those that had died there, and that it needed a feng shui master to clear the 'bad energy and let their souls move on and be cleansed'. I can only say that it was the unhappiest place that my family had stayed in, in all the years of moving around Hong Kong.

Our first Christmas was coming up, but one day my father came back home looking upset and miserable—he had received news from the UK that Nana had passed away. I only heard this from my mother because she told me that my father was too upset to tell you kids. My mother was also very upset as if she had lost a close aunt, and this news dampened the merriment of the Christmas festivities. Nana had always expressed her last wish to her son before she died that he could arrange for her to visit us in Hong Kong and spend a Christmas with the family—in fact, she had hardly ever been out of the UK, never mind the East! Yet since the last leave we had in the UK, in Southampton in 1969, my mother told me that not once did he call her or return the letters that she wrote to him. My father had not really been in contact with Nana since the leave in 1965 in her house in South Shields. We were all very upset, and my mother said, 'I tried to comfort your father and said how sorry I am. I said to him I will miss Nana. Why don't you take some leave, go back, and see your sister and the rest of your family?'

My father's response was an abrupt 'What do you know? I will handle it and leave it to me!'

As much as my mother wanted to offer him support in her own way, he was a stubborn old Geordie and rejected help in any way. Quite clearly, my father had not forgiven Nana after all these years and had almost treated his mother as if she was no longer alive. Apparently, he did telephone his sister, Mable, back in North Shields and shared his grief over the telephone with her but still resisted the need for him to fly back for the funeral. Nana died of bronchial complications as she had smoked right up to her last days. She was nearly seventy years old. I think that that was the last blow my father could take in his life, and once that happened, he felt that there was not much future for him. Slowly, his confidence of looking after the family diminished. He hit the bottle even more intensely (as a way of handling his grief), and around this time, he finally admitted to my mother that he was an alcoholic and that it was killing him. My mother even told me that his superior officer (Superintendent Mike) would recommend that he take early retirement and move on with his life. By this time, he was nearly approaching twenty years of service in the force, and in those days, the pension benefits were quite generous. However, knowing what a proud Geordie man he was, he would've liked to pick his time to say goodbye, rather than being surreptitiously forced to go.

My precocious little sister came out with a remark one afternoon when we were in the playground, 'I think Mum and Dad don't like each other. Mum wants a divorce.' I didn't understand what a divorce meant until she explained to me that it happens when two people don't want to live together any more.

I asked her, 'So what's going to happen to us?'

She just shrugged her shoulders and went off to play with her friend, Tina. Yet if that ever came to be, I knew which parent I would stay with. I recall a very ominous sign, a premonition as I could best describe it, which came to me to underline how serious my parents were loathing each other. We were able to sense how bad the vibes between them were. My mother said that I had started talking in my dreams and was suffering from nasty nightmares at least a couple of times a week. However, this time it was more than a nightmare when my mother found me sleepwalking from my bedroom all the way to the bathroom. She said she followed me to the bathroom and was careful not to wake me. She was trying to guide me back to the bedroom, when I suddenly yelled at her saying, 'Leave my father alone. You are going to harm him!'

She was absolutely shocked and frightened, because I had my eyes closed, and I had picked up a razor blade from the bathroom to try to slash my mother! Fortunately, she was able to control me, and she gently led me back to the bedroom. I would not be able to offer an explanation nor could my mother, but alas, events in the near future were to prove it was not a joke! After twelve years of a turbulent marriage and all that happened, I could see now that my parents were not going to last the course. I suppose the only reason they stayed together was because of us kids, and the strain did not help the marriage either. My brother in the meantime, would lock himself in his own room (I no longer shared his room, and now I was sharing a bed with my father) and had an ambivalent attitude to the marital strife—but he knew what was going on with my parents.

With the atmosphere in our Ho Man Tin apartment getting more and more fraught between my parents, my father, when he was sober, was able to see how damaging it was for the children to see grown adults trading insults and seeing such confrontation. I had missed seeing my best friend, Paul, in Happy Valley, and this was the perfect excuse for me to get away from all the tension and spend alternate weekends with him and his family—my father wholeheartedly agreed to this arrangement. For the next six months or so, I would spend every two weekends a month at Paul's in Race Course Mansions, right opposite Happy Valley Racecourse and the football field!

Paul's family represented the complete opposite family structure that I had come from. They were kind and gentle; the parents Auntie Millie and Uncle Toto were so soft spoken to each other, and the general ambience of the home was peaceful and loving—and there wasn't a whiff of alcohol around their home. Paul was the only son of the family. He was, dare I say it, the favourite and spoilt by his parents. Auntie Millie and Uncle

Toto treated me like their second son and understood the difficulties surrounding my parents. I remember Auntie Millie calling me into her room one day, wanting to say something important to me. She gently said, 'I am sorry that your parents are arguing so much, and it causes you so much unhappiness, dear Peter. But these things do happen between adults. I want to let you know that you are always welcome to stay with Paul and us as long as your parents don't mind. Paul likes you so much and says you are his best friend.' Even my own mother never spoke to me this way! Then Auntie Millie changed her caring and kind expression into a more stern approach and added, 'As long as you and Paul do your homework and be good at school, agreed?'

I nodded fervently and gave her a hug. Her stern look suddenly changed, and she cheekily gave me wink! I can look back with extreme gratitude at Paul and his family that this offer from Paul's parents was such a help in limiting the emotional damage that could be caused by having to see the clashes between my father and mother. My sister was also given an opportunity to get away. She was allowed to stay with Auntie Rita where she became friends with her daughter Shirley. For my brother, who was a keen boy scout, I think he used weekends and every weekend to go out with his fellow scouts or just hang out with his Chinese friends. I had lost touch with Paul after what happened and sadly found out years later that he passed away in California in 1997, at only thirty-nine years of age. He was always large-sized from the first day I knew him, and his sister Kathy, who now lives in New York, told me that he died of a heart attack. His mother, Auntie Millie, discovered his body at home where he had collapsed, and she has never really recovered from that trauma of seeing her son die like that. I wanted to catch up with Auntie Millie and Uncle Toto (they have retired and live in California) to thank them in person for caring for me so much during those times, but Kathy told me that it would be too painful for them to see me as I would remind them of their son, Paul. Such kind and loving people like that didn't deserve such a cruel hand of fate!

According to my mother, she made one last effort to get my father some help for his drinking, his anger, and she thought, his depressive state. She really came to the conclusion that even if the marriage could not be saved, he could save himself if he would at least try for some of the sessions with the police welfare officer and talk things through. In 1971, I am pretty sure, that 'talk therapy' was still in its infancy in Hong Kong, and its effectiveness in dealing with personal issues was limited. The welfare officer did explain to my mother that the service would help the individual come to terms with the issues rather than running away from it or masking it with various forms of addictive substances. My mother said that she would take any help to solve the crisis. The result of this last effort was more abuse and threats from my father to her. He shouted, 'If I go to hell, I will do it my way!'

Clearly, it sounded like he was a very disturbed man. One frightening instance that my sister and I had witnessed of his worsening condition was on one Saturday when he picked us from a school outing. He had already been drinking because as soon as we got into the car we could smell it. Then as we drove off towards home, we could see that his driving and coordination was all over the place, with the car dangerously swerving all over Waterloo Road on the way back to Ho Man Tin. I shouted at my father, 'Dad, don't drive so fast. We're scared you might crash the car!'

Luckily, for all of us, the road was unusually traffic free, as otherwise Waterloo road is the main arterial road connecting traffic from the New

Territories to Kowloon. We both started to cry, and then he suddenly shouted to us in the back seat, 'Get out of the car, you kids! Walk home, walk home.'

He had realised that he could endanger our lives by crashing on the central barrier or on to the oncoming traffic. The car screeched to a halt just outside the Hoover Restaurant on Waterloo Road, one his local favourites restaurants where we had many dim sum lunches and evening dinners. We jumped out still crying and wondered what would happen to our father, and then just saw a trail of exhaust smoke spitting out of the car as he sped off in the direction of Yau Ma Tei. Some local people recognised us and came to over to see if we were all right.

I remember one newsagent, whom my father got newspapers from, saying something like, 'Oh, your father drink too much, very sad! You OK? Do you need me to take you back to Ho Man Tin?'

Still crying, we both said we could manage to walk home. To comfort ourselves we went into the local ParknShop at the bottom of Ho Man Tin hill and bought ourselves some ice cream—it was just what we needed. When we reached home, we immediately told our mother about what had happened, and her reaction was more of horror than being upset about what had happened. She could not restrain her anger and resentment towards my father now. 'He is no good as a father, for us or himself!' she yelled in the kitchen.

We did not see him after that and for the rest of the weekend.

The Night That Changed Our Lives Forever

The summer of 1971 and leading into the autumn was one of the wettest and one of the stormiest seasons we had experienced in my memory of Hong Kong. I recall that for the months from August to October, there were at least five typhoons all at signal eight and above, which meant that we had our school cancelled and had to be locked indoors—very boring! Torrential rain caused floods all over the place, with trees broken like toothpicks and falling on to roads, blocking all traffic. Ho Man Tin was on quite a steep hill, so whenever the heavy rains came, the whole of Ho Man Tin Street would be flooded, and we would be cut off for a few days. I wondered how all those neon signs in Nathan Road and Mong Kok stayed precariously hanging on to the side of the buildings by a thread of wire, nuts, and bolts. To me, those signs looked like a tonne of glass and metal that must have been extremely dangerous to anybody walking near them if they fell (actually rarely)! One thing I noticed that whenever there was a severe typhoon, there was an eerie silence and quiet about Hong Kong. The streets were left deserted, all the shops boarded up, trees and leaves strewn across the once busy roads, and not a person in sight—but the neon lights were still on! I asked my mother, 'What do Chinese people do when they have to stay at home and are not able to walk in the streets to do their shopping?'

She shrugged her shoulders and meekly replied, 'Maybe they play mah-jong.'

Money was tight. My father's drinking was expensive, and he ran up unpaid bills of hundreds of dollars in the officer's mess, which my mother had to pay on his behalf—a great loss of face for my mother. My father gave my mother $500 per month to cover all the food and household expenses, and this, she said, was a struggle to do every month. My mother was a good saver, sometimes too good—something she had learnt from her poor background—and had always put away a healthy amount for a 'rainy day', whereas my father was pretty hopeless! Arguments between them often centred round money, and he would complain and resent giving the money to my mother. Her reaction would be 'I don't want your lousy money' as she would yell back at him. Christmas was approaching, and by judging the tension between them, it was not going to be a joyous occasion. It had been raining heavily for most of the day, and, in fact, the newspapers confirmed that December was the wettest ever in sixty years.

Something very strange and ominous happened on the evening of 19 December 1971, which my mother has never forgotten. She recalled that my father had finished work early and had come home first. Behind the front door, from where someone entered the apartment, there was a large wall mirror facing you, and underneath it, the telephone and a chair were kept. That day, when my father entered the flat, my mother said she caught a glimpse of my father looking into the mirror as he entered—what she saw was like something out of horror movie!

'For a split second', she said, 'I saw the complexion of his face change completely into an ashen dull grey colour, totally different from his usual pink blushed colour. It was like he was dead or as if he was a ghost!'

Whenever she recalled the moment, she said she felt terrified, almost as if the 'Angel of Death' had arrived for my father. Once he entered the living room, his usual colour returned. The signs were ominous it would seem—surreal like the film *The Amityville Horror*. My father decided to take my sister and I to the Hoover Restaurant for a Christmas meal (and it was indeed the last meal we would have together) but my mother and were not invited. On the way home, my father asked me to get some more beer from the ParknShop, which I did buy for him, and with the rain coming down even heavier, we just wanted to get inside and go to bed. When we got back inside, the rains became torrential and now with the deafening sound of thunder and lightning, the atmosphere was distinctly disturbing. I saw my mother in full solitude, watching television, and beside her chair was a glass filled with some wine or brandy. She did not acknowledge us when we came in and seemed tense and nervous, not saying anything to anyone and sat in a very rigid posture. It was almost nine in the evening, so it was bedtime for us, and our father marched us into bed and gave us a goodnight hug. I could see he was tense as well, and in the way he walked out of the bedroom, he seemed to be preparing himself for a long night! My mother recalled that she was desperate to get out of the flat and leave my father on his own, but with the rain so heavy, she thought that 'she felt that she was trapped there'. She wanted to avoid trouble that night and could have asked the neighbours to let her stay a few hours, but it was late. Not only that, but having to escape from the husband and losing face with the rather 'gossiping neighbours' was just something she could not do at that moment. Within ten minutes, I was fast asleep, and I would always unconsciously sleep to one side of the bed, leaving space for my father for him to get into bed when he was ready.

Between the hours of nine thirty to midnight, in those crucial two and half hours, something significant must've happened between my parents. The next thing I knew was my father uncharacteristically rushing into the bedroom (usually he was quiet not to disturb my sleep) and was anxious and tense, and he was breathing heavily as if he had done something strenuous. The bedroom light was suddenly switched on, and I awoke and saw my mother rushing in with a fury and rage on her face and her hair all rustled up and untidy. I can never forget the moment I saw in her eyes this strange glaze totally fixated on my father—she was after him. Then, like a flash, I saw in her right hand the shiny reflection of the blade of the knife as she rushed round the bed to where my father was standing. My father almost begged my mother, 'Please, Vicky, I am sorry. I am sorry, I didn't mean it. Please don't do this!'

In one clean jab, my mother plunged the knife into my father's abdomen, and then he fell to the floor. My mother rushed out just as quick as she had come in. I was still in bed, totally in shock, sitting up on the bed, seeing my father writhing in pain. Blood from his abdomen was pouring on to the shiny wooden floor, and he began yelling in pain. I just froze. I was still probably half-asleep and so stunned by the rapidity of events. Then suddenly my mother entered the room again and very oddly laid the knife under the bed. The knife seemed cleaned of blood, and then she walked straight out—she probably thought that my father was exaggerating his pain. I really was a spectator to all this, and totally powerless to do anything—just paralysed! My father's pains had become more intense, and he started shouting, 'Vicky, Vicky, Vicky, it really hurts, help me, please!'

Then hearing all this commotion, my brother came into the room, went straight over to my father, and opened his shirt to see the wound (I think he had some first aid training in the boy scouts). He seemed to be trying to stem the bleeding as he was pressing on the area of the wound.

The smell in the air in the bedroom had suddenly been overcome with my father's perspiration and now his bowels had failed him—it was horrible. From that moment, everything else seemed a blur. I was too shocked to do anything or say anything to my father, and somehow I left the bedroom with my brother still tending to the wound—there was now a pool of blood on the floor. I managed to walk into the living room where my mother was just sitting, the television off, just sitting there in her private thoughts, still with her glass of something half full. She said nothing, and did not acknowledge me at all. The next thing I knew was that 999 was called by my brother, and my sister was sitting next to our mother. It seemed to take forever for the ambulance to arrive, probably due to the inclement weather, and when it did, my father was almost unconscious and had already lost a lot of blood. Following the police, the ambulance men had finally arrived carrying a huge stretcher with them. I could hear in the background their voices saying in their colloquial Cantonese that they were struggling to lift my father on to the stretcher and that he was a 'big fat gweilo', and how bad he smelt. When I saw them carrying out my father, they were perspiring profusely and were now wearing masks. We were told that he would be taken to the Queen Elizabeth Hospital and that if we wanted to come to the hospital we would have to arrange other transport.

Events were happening fast, especially in my father's condition. The delay of the ambulance meant that my father was bleeding more and had lost a lot of blood. To complicate his condition, he had been drinking at least half a dozen bottles of San Miguel, which meant that there was too much alcohol in his blood for the doctors to operate on him. According to the night duty doctor, he advised that they had to wait until the alcohol in his blood would clear before any surgery could be done on him. The danger now was that he was bleeding internally as more time went by. The time now was well in the early hours of 20 December, and my mother suggested that we go to the hospital and see his latest condition—it was not a pretty sight. We were allowed entry into the intensive care room that he was staying in, and from a small window, I saw my father lying in bed with an intravenous drip, seemingly coming in and out of consciousness. The distressing moment for me was when I saw my father becoming delusional, ripping off the intravenous drip, and yelling at the nurses, 'Leave me alone, get away from me!' The nurses rushed in to calm him down but could not handle him. They had to call for more back-up, and eventually, somehow, they sedated him. My mother kept saying, 'Harry, will be all right. It was only a small wound.'

Some six hours had passed, and it was finally decided that they had to operate on him because of the serious internal bleeding from the stab wound. As my father was wheeled to the operating theatre, and we entered the lift, the last words I heard my father utter were to my brother. He was saying, '. . . look after the kids . . . look after the kids.' It seemed that my father had given up his fight for life and knew that he may not make it through the operation. I vaguely heard my brother reply with something of an 'OK', but I could see his fear and trepidation on such a responsibility—I felt for him!

My mother stood in the corner of the lift, remaining silent, and I was just in a daze but witnessing everything. I have always regretted that I did not speak to my father and say some comforting words—I was just scared. By this time, the number of uniformed police officers arrived and one or two British adults whom I recall as my father's senior officers called Mike were in the waiting room. Less than two hours later, one of the doctors came out and announced to us that my father had lost his life on the operating table. I cannot recall accurately my reaction, but in all the subsequent years of coming to terms with this tragedy, I did have flashbacks of what I experienced. The only way I could describe my reaction was an emptiness in my world, a void, a sort of complete disorientation and confusion. I could hear in the distance that my mother's reaction was one of absolute shock.

'What? Harry dead? Oh no! Oh no!'

The news was eventually relayed to the officers present. I could see that Mike looked quite shocked, and his head dropped in disappointment. At that point, the officers moved swiftly towards my mother, surrounded her, and moved her in the direction of a private room down the hospital corridor. I had no idea where they were taking her. After some time, suddenly the door opened, and one of the officers was holding my mother's arm and leading her out of the room, followed by the others—I did not see any handcuffs. I just could not believe my eyes in what I was seeing, and I sensed that they were taking her away from me and that I may not see her again for some time. I caught a brief glimpse of my mother's face and saw a woman that looked totally bewildered, stunned, and resigned to the fact that she was responsible for the fatal incident. It was as if all life had been drained out of her, and her eyes just gazed ahead as if she was a blind person. I cried and said something like, 'Mum, don't go. Please don't take my mum away!'

She probably could not hear me and did not glance back at us. I was told by the hospital staff that my mother was to taken down to Kowloon City Police Station and would be interviewed and questioned by the officers about the night's events. I knew though that my mother had committed a serious crime and would face charges. It was confirmed later, as we went back to Ho Man Tin, that my mother was now under arrest for the stabbing of my father and would be charged with murder. I had managed to get the official copy of the police statement/ report in which Senior Inspector Chan, at two twenty-five hours on 20 December 1971, had formally charged my mother with murder. The statement read:

'You Ng Hung also known as Mrs Vicky Victoria Craggs made a statement to DPC (Detective Police Constable) Cheng at 02.30 hours on the 19 December 1971, in which you described the incident occurred earlier that day between you and your husband, Mr Harry Craggs, and in that statement you stated that you had stabbed your husband. Your husband died this morning. I now arrest you for killing your husband.

'You are not obliged to say anything unless you wish to do so, and whatever you say will be taken down in writing and may be given in evidence.'

My mother made a reply:

'He was drunk. I had also taken some wine. I had completely no intent to kill him.'

By lunchtime, on 20 December 1971, my world and the life that we had been living changed dramatically—we were now like orphans. In just over twenty-four hours, my former identity with the Craggs family had been completely destroyed when my poor mother in less than ten minutes of confrontation with my father had plunged that instrument into his abdomen. News travelled fast in the Ho Man Tin neighbourhood, especially in high-rise block of flats, and with the police and other officials moving in and out of Flat 23, people were wandering around downstairs in the car park and figuring out that something serious had happened to the Craggs family. Some of my mother's acquaintances came around to the flat to offer us dinner and take us out of the rather haunted atmosphere of our former home, and I did take up the offer. Yet I could sense that they were wary of helping us too much because of the usual Chinese superstitions. They thought that getting involved in a family tragedy of ours would rub off on them too!

By the next day, 21 December, the news had already been reported in the two leading newspapers—the *South China Morning Post* and *The Standard, Hong Kong*—that Inspector Harry Craggs had been murdered by his Chinese wife, Vicky Ng Hung Victoria Craggs (see newspaper cut-outs). We had become the most famous police family in Hong Kong and for all the wrong reasons!

Relief from the unwanted media attention came to my sister and me—I got a phone call from Paul, who, on the advice of his mother, Auntie Millie, suggested I stay with them until all the publicity had died down. My sister was offered to stay at Auntie Rita's and her children. We both jumped at the opportunity of getting out of this scenario, and we were to move as far as possible from that area and go back to Hong Kong Island. It was time to say goodbye to Ho Man Tin and to all that brief experience of living there as the Craggs family, and also say goodbye to Kowloon Side, where we were not to return again for the foreseeable future.

Clearly, the sudden death of my father in such a situation still had a numbing affect on me. I was to learn many years later that my father was to be buried in the Hong Kong cemetery in Happy Valley, which is famous for the burial of colonial serving personnel from HM Forces. It was absolutely incredible to see hundreds upon hundreds of gravestones of British servicemen, some as young as seventeen, who had lost their lives in this part of the world to maintain the British Empire! My sister and I were not invited to go to the funeral and the burial of my father's coffin, probably to protect us from all the sadness and trauma, but my brother, at seventeen years of age, was considered mature enough to represent the family. According to the keeper of the cemetery, who I spoke to and who remembered the day of the burial, he had never seen such a large hearse and colleagues in attendance for the burial for all the years he had been working there—some recognition for my father from his colleagues in the police force I suppose! My mother told me that he wanted to be buried under a tree so he could have some shade from the sun—and that's exactly what he got from the position of the burial site at Hong Kong cemetery, right underneath a coconut tree! I had to be careful every time I visited my father's grave and make sure there were no coconuts dangling precariously over me, in case one fell on my head, and that may be the end of me as well! The fact that we had not been invited to see our father buried and recognise and come to terms with the fact that we had lost our father—the term is closure—was very damaging to me in the subsequent years of growing up as an adult in the UK. I am amazed in myself that it was not until 1983, on my first return trip to Hong Kong as a young undergraduate, that I had seen my father's tombstone—some twelve years after his death!

In the psychiatric and counselling profession, the grieving process and acknowledging the loss was a natural and healthy way of dealing with bereavement, and yet I was denied that opportunity until many years later so that I could move on with my life. I had particularly felt it acutely since I was the closest to my father in the latter years of his life and that this pivotal parental relationship was taken away from me at a crucial adolescent age of twelve years of age. After all, I had seen the full horror of the incident with my own eyes—and the only one! Eventually, over the years, I got the courage and tenacity to seek some professional help in finally having complete closure on this, but not after it had wreaked havoc on my emotional and physical development, over the years, while growing up as a teenager and as a young adult in London, UK.

Trial by Media and the Trial in the Supreme Court of Hong Kong

So what had really happened on that night that led to all this? I know that both my parents were very unhappy with each other, that arguments were more frequent, and my father was drinking more. That word 'divorce' was mentioned quite a lot between them, and I had finally understood what that meant when Auntie Millie explained it to me. Even after nearly forty years since the trial of my mother, I was still curious about the details of the trial, the issues involved, and about what had really happened. As I cast my memory back to all those people, faces, places, and what I observed as a twelve-year-old boy, they are still distinctly crystal clear and quite fresh in my mind right now! I had always wondered though if I could trace the official court papers of the case from the Hong Kong Supreme Court, since with such widespread coverage in the press and media, it was a high-profile case of a slain British police officer by his Chinese wife. I think my natural curiosity from being trained in the broadcast media myself, and the research skills I had learnt in that profession, gave me the motivation and perseverance to press on and see how much could I find—the breakthrough came in the summer of 2009.

The Hong Kong Central Library is the main official public library and is located directly opposite Victoria Park. It is almost equidistant from Causeway Bay and Tin Hau Station. It's an impressive modern building that rises to eight floors, and the design and layout is remarkably spacious and relaxing, considering its location. I was advised that the library keeps archives of most of Hong Kong's media publications, and certainly had back copies of the two main papers namely the *South China Morning Post* (*SCMP*) and *The Standard, Hong Kong*. Further enquiries led me to the microfilm section on the sixth floor where I was informed that all archives of the print media were kept there, and indeed they kept all print media material, going back to WWII. My mind was ticking away fast, and I could feel the adrenalin rushing through me and the excitement of seeing what was written about the case and pictures (if any) that were published—I was not disappointed!

Fortunately, I could remember the month and the date of the incident, so I did not have to go through a mass of microfilm reels to scroll through for the stories on my parents' case. With the box of some half a dozen reels given to me by the helpful and courteous staff, I sat myself down in the most secluded part of the area, composed myself, and made sure I had some water with me (officially no drinks allowed there), looked at the reels, and hesitated for some strange reason. I had come this far and had made this effort, and yet, inside me, the little voice kept saying to me, 'Hey, Peter, do you really want to read this stuff? It might be too painful and bring all that s—t back!'

I sat there, I think, for at least ten minutes, wondering if I should start this, and looking around, I was seeing other people enthusiastically scrolling through the reels, glued to their screens, reading and muttering to themselves about what they were researching. Behind me, there was an impressive view of Victoria Park and beyond that, I could see the harbour and Kowloon Side, and as it was getting darker, the glistening lights of the office buildings and hotels were flashing pleasantly, lifting my spirits somewhat. With that spark of encouragement, I took a deep breath, refocused my attention on the box of reels, and loaded them. The film made the usual winding and swishing noise while moving through the machine parts. I knew what date I was looking for—it was either 20 or 21 December 1971, and with the controls, I was able to speed up the scrolling or slow it down as I went through *SCMP* and *The Standard*. I wasn't sure whether the news of my father's death would be on the front page of either newspapers, so I was meticulous in scanning through the first five pages of the paper. I was amazed to read about some of the news headlines and about how Hong Kong's link to the UK was still a very strong one.

On 21 December, on the front page of the *The Standard* there it was—a younger looking picture of my father next to the story of Zulfikar Ali Bhutto, who was elected prime minister of Pakistan after thirteen years of military rule of the country. As I was reading the story of the killing of my father, I burst into tears!,

The headline in the Standard read: 'Wife accused of killing policeman'

'A mother-of-three was remanded for three days on a charge of killing her police prosecutor husband, C H Craggs. Vicky Victoria Craggs nee Ng Hung of Ho Man Tin, Kowloon, was alleged to have killed her husband on Sunday morning. According to police, the killing followed a row. Inspector Craggs was stabbed in the stomach several times. He was admitted to Queen Elizabeth Hospital where he died the same day. Inspector Craggs joined the force in August 1952. Before his death, he was officer-in-charge of the South Kowloon Magistracy. A police officer said Inspector Craggs,

43, was 'a nice man to work with'. He said, 'He worked hard and got along well with everyone in the office.'

As I was scanning through the news of the two main newspapers, I had found that the Standard had much more comphrensive coverage than that of the SCMP, hence I have decided to quote directly from their news articles about the death of my father. Eventually I composed myself and managed to read and reread to absorb this information. It was the first time in nearly forty years that I had seen this, and of course in all that time, there was no one in the immediate family or former friends of my father to tell me about this and how it was reported in the newspapers. I suppose at that particular time in my life I was ready to face the facts and see for myself the whole drama unfold before me—all in a public library in Hong Kong. I drank a lot of water! There was more to come, and scrolling through the months, I came across more news coverage about the case, although from the time of the death of my father, from December 1971 to February 1972, there was a gap in the news as my mother was in the Tai Lam Chung Women's Prison, awaiting trial for murder. On 24 February, *The Standard* reported on page 5 in the section Hong Kong Focus:

'Wife denies murder.' The Chinese wife of a European police inspector at the criminal sessions in the Supreme Court yesterday denied murdering her husband.'

The trial for murder against my mother had officially opened at the Supreme Court properly in March 1972, and by this time, she had been incarcerated for nearly three months. The awe of reading this and taking it all in became too much for me in one afternoon and evening session in the library, and having been through all sorts of emotions in absorbing this material, I had to have a break from reading more about the reporters' story of the trial. To my delight, I was allowed to photocopy all the reported stories in the papers and even the library staff was surprised about how many copies I wanted!

On 14 March, the *SCMP* continued with its reporting of the case with the headline of a 'Bargirl that was charged with murder' . . .

I must admit that I felt hurt and insulted by the *SCMP's* report that called my mother a 'bargirl', since she was not working and had not worked in that area for well over fifteen years. One of the more revealing reports of the case came a week later in *The Standard*:

'I was treated worse than a housemaid, says Craggs's wife'

'Vicky Victoria Craggs, formerly known as Ng Hung, 44, who has denied murdering her husband, Police Inspector Charles Henry Craggs, told the Supreme Court yesterday that her husband treated her 'worse than a housemaid'.

'. . . She told Chief Justice, Sir Ivo Rigby, and a jury of five men and two women that she married Inspector Craggs in 1958. Two months after their marriage, she became pregnant, but her husband was not happy about it, Mrs Craggs said. In their married life, her husband never treated her as a wife, but treated her worse than a housemaid. He always got drunk and came home late, and kicked her, scolded her, and called her a prostitute. He also threatened to 'fix her up' she said by sending her to a mental hospital, or to jail, or back to China. Mrs Craggs said she had sought assistance from a police welfare officer and a psychiatrist, but there was no improvement . . .'

I was totally enthralled and absorbed by this report, because for the first time, I was able to see what my parents' relationship was like, and certainly painted a picture of my father in a dark light. Quite clearly, my mother was trying her best to portray herself as a victim of this alcoholic husband, and that she had been fighting for survival. Reading this did give me a more tainted impression of my loving father, and I concluded that he was quite an ill man, living with a woman he did not love any more. On 24 March, another report appeared in *The Standard*:

'I heard Craggs cry in pain'

'Vicky Victoria Craggs told the Supreme Court yesterday that she did not know she had stabbed her husband, Inspector Craggs until he cried out in pain . . . . Mrs Craggs said that her husband was stabbed in a 'scuffle' with her on the early morning of December 19 following a quarrel . . . . Mrs Craggs said that on December 18, her husband returned home from work at about 3.00 p.m., and when she kissed him, she smelt alcohol on this breath. Inspector Craggs then gave her $500 to buy Christmas presents for the children. Mrs Craggs told the children that they would go out and buy them some other time because it was raining heavily. Inspector Craggs drank another six large bottles of beer while watching television and later went to sleep, Mrs Craggs said. He woke up at about 6.00 p.m., and the whole family went out for a meal in a restaurant in Waterloo Road. On the way home, he told his eldest son, Peter, to buy five large bottles of beer. At home, he watched TV and drank more beer. After a while, he started in a low voice, Mrs Craggs said. He called himself a 'fool' because he gave money to his wife instead of using the money to have a 'good time' in the Tsim Sha Tsui or Wan Chai area, Mrs Craggs said. He also complained that she did not thank him when he gave her the money and that he was treated like a 'sucker'. She returned the money to him and asked him not to grumble any more. She told him to use the money for his enjoyment. He called her a 'prostitute' and said that she was 'worse than a bargirl'. And she slapped him. She ran into the kitchen and later went into her husband's room. She was so frightened that she did not know what she was doing. Her husband again called her a prostitute, and she scuffled with him. During the fight, she felt some object come into contact with his body, and she withdrew her hand. She said she did not know that her husband was stabbed until he cried out loud in pain. He then fell to the floor bleeding. She asked her son, Peter, to call for an ambulance and dial 999. An ambulance arrived about forty-five minutes later. Mrs Craggs said that she had been frequently beaten up and threatened by her husband since 1962. She had to see a family doctor twice a week and took tranquillisers to help her to go to sleep at night. Her husband often went to sleep on returning home from work and woke up about midnight. He would then start grumbling and pick on her. Sometimes after needling her, he would make love to her and then would cool down, Mrs Craggs said. When he was off duty, he would drink heavily and threaten her. Sometimes she had to sleep in the back staircase landing to keep away from him until he went to sleep, she said. The hearing continues today.'

Again, this was a revelation to me because for the first time I could read about what my parents' relationship was like and account for the events of what happened that night—I was still in tears. Going through all of this was almost like being transported back to that time, except for the fact that I could see that I was an innocent naive son in a very dysfunctional family environment and unaware of the tension between these two people. Luckily, the library had a coffee shop downstairs, where I took frequent breaks from reading the intensity and emotions of the story! With the momentum gained from the newspaper archives, I was motivated now to trace the original court papers to the case in the Supreme Court. When I approached the High Court enquiries, they initially told me that any case longer than thirty years was destroyed and that would be the end of the matter. However, having this intuitive persistence of mine which kept goading me along (or maybe my father's presence) I made further enquires to the Hong Kong Records Office based in Kwun Tong, and there I found the information that eluded me from the High Court. I was truly amazed!

I saw, for the first time in my adult life, the contract of employment that my father had with the Hong Kong Police Force, his stipend and conditions of service, and the precise dates of when he started in the force to the day of his death. Wearing gloves (compulsory) to protect the original papers (dated 1952), I gently, and at times emotionally, read through the literature to form a nostalgic picture of my father's early days in the Crown Colony and could see how the British administration had been set up in Hong Kong. It was surreal, as if I had been cast back in time to those days! The trail of information did not end there—what about all the court proceedings and the people involved? More success was just around the corner, and at last, I was able to find the reference number and date relating to the court case on the database. There it was— HCCC (High Court Criminal Case) Case No. 8 of 1972, the record office and the High Court still had the papers to the case! You can imagine my heart beginning to pound faster with excitement but also a kind of trepidation about all that happened. I was told by the High Court Registry that paper records of criminal cases were never destroyed and were kept with the registry indefinitely—hallelujah! Following protocol, I had to write to the chief clerk of the registry and explain to them the reasons why I would like to have access to the court papers. My persistence paid off, and as I truly believe with some help from another source (probably my father's presence), they accepted my request and granted me access to the papers. In the heart of the impressive Pacific Place shopping plaza, the Hong Kong High Court offices occupied an adjacent building, predictably the familiar grey government buildings that reached at least ten-storey high—the usual Hong Kong convenience and efficiency!

I was impressed that the paper records of the case were in pretty good condition. The clerk to the registry was very understanding of my request and was kind enough to give me a private room for me to have the privacy to do my research. She even commented that I had done extremely well to trace all this information and that it was very rare that anyone would have access to such confidential papers. I think I impressed her because I had mentioned the names of quite a few well-known legal professionals that were involved in my mother's case—Sir Ivo Rigby, Helen A Lo, and Miles Jackson-Lipkin, and she knew all of them! I amazed myself that after nearly forty years since the trial I was able to remember the names of the main players in the trial, and with the papers right in front of me, I was pretty accurate in my recollection of events.

I was the key and only witness in seeing my mother stab my father in the stomach on the night of 19 December 1971. Although I was twelve years of age, by law I was officially of legal age to stand and give evidence in court that would have some bearing on the outcome of my mother's fate. By mid-January 1972, when the case had come to the Supreme court, my mother had been incarcerated at Tai Lam Chung Women's Detention Centre for nearly a month. Media and newspaper coverage had been established and that news of the trial would be reported regularly (about every two weeks). As one would expect of a youngster, I was not aware of the impressive line-up for the case of prosecution and defence in the courthouse. Sir Ivo Rigby, a well-known and highly respected chief justice of the High Court, would be presiding over the proceedings. Counsel for the defence was yet-to-be-famous and rather eccentric barrister, Miles Jackson-Lipkin QC (some more about him later) hired by Helen A Lo, the well-known family solicitor that my mother had sought legal advice from over the years. Counsel for prosecution was A. P. Duckett. All the court proceedings were held in the Supreme Court of Hong Kong, which looks like a mini-St Paul's, with its dome that stood out from the rest of the high-rise office buildings of the business area in the heart of Chater Road Central (now it is used for the Hong Kong SAR LegCo sittings).

Throughout the my mother's case, my sister and I were able to sit in the public gallery and watch what was going on, and the court ushers came to know us as the children of the woman on trial. Under the circumstances, school was no longer a priority for me, and it was arranged with Auntie Millie's help that my attendance at the Island School would be suspended until the outcome of the case. Each morning, the proceedings would start at ten o'clock. There in the darkened corner, with a court usher on one side of her and a security guard on the other side, would sit my demure mother, looking straight ahead at the judge, clutching to what looked like a handkerchief or tissue. She would sit with her head bowed, sobbing intermittently—a sight that I had become more used to as time went by. I can recall that in all the time of the case, we had at least gone to hear the case two to three times a week, and the primary reason for me to go was to make sense of what had befallen our family, my parents, and what this all meant to me. Since my sister was staying in Blue Pool Road with Auntie Rita, which was our last residence before the move to Ho Man Tin, and I was staying in Happy Valley, it was easy for us to meet up, travel to Central by tram, and attend the court hearings. The formalities of the court were quite rigid. Especially when Judge Ivo Rigby entered the courthouse, someone would announce 'All rise for the presiding judge, Sir Ivo Rigby'.

Sometimes my sister and I would snigger at the funny hats and costumes they were wearing, especially the judge who wore the traditional white wig that seemed to be too small for his head!. The court itself reminded me of a church interior, with a lot of bland wooden furniture and the smell to go with it. To the right of where we were sitting in the public gallery was the formal seating arrangement for the jury to sit, and from there they could see my mother from across the court when she was in the dock. To our left from the gallery marched in the eccentric Miles Jackson-Lipkin QC, also with the funny wig on and his gown that seemed hanging to his body like a large black blanket. I remember quite clearly how his voice would boom around the court and seem too loud for the listening witnesses and the public gallery. He was quite an animated character, always gesticulating with his hands to make salient points, and from what I could gather, passionately pleading with the jury about the hard times my mother had to endure in the marriage to my father. On the other hand, Counsel for Prosecution A. P. Duckett was almost the direct opposite of Jackson-Lipkin—dour, restrained, monotone in voice, and seemed very officious. I know that I much preferred the style of Jackson-Lipkin to Mr Duckett—after all, he was defending my mother against a murder charge!

At the time of my mother's trial in early 1972, Miles Jackson-Lipkin was a well-respected and highly regarded barrister in Hong Kong. He was already quite well known for his style and eccentric behaviour, and because of this he had attracted some attention from of the print media.

Commentators were describing his lifestyle as something like coming out of a novel, when at the height of his career in the 1970s and 80s, it was reported that he needed assistance of two chauffeured automobiles to reach his office. Apparently the then colonial government provided one Rolls Royce to deliver his briefcase, and the other Rolls to drive him to court!

His undoubted skills and ability led to his rapid rise and promotion to become a judge a few years later after my mother's case. Just as the speed of his elevation to the highest position in the legal profession made news in Hong Kong, his eccentric and lavish lifestyle would eventually cause an even more famous downfall in his status. The beginning of his downfall started when it was discovered that he had not given his true birth date to the authorities and that his claim to his rank in the Royal Navy and awards for military service were not genuinely earned by himself.

Many years after his retirement, the authorities had caught up with Jackson-Lipkin and his wife, Barrister Lucille Fung Yung-Shum and discovered they had been fraudulently over-claiming welfare payments from the Hong Kong government. They were finally convicted in January 2007 on three counts of welfare fraud and sentenced to eleven months jail sentence, the first judge in Hong Kong's history to be convicted of a criminal charge. A rather ignominious ending to an illustrious career! However, in the days that I attended the trial, I was able to have a brief encounter with Mr Jackson-Lipkin in court. I remember him saying to me, 'It's most unfortunate for you and your family to have to go through this, and I do hope we can get the best outcome for your mother and all of you in your family.'

My impression of Mr Jackson-Lipkin was that he was a kind man who was really determined to help us through this trauma and reunite us as a family as soon as possible. What he had said to me in that one encounter was the best encouragement I could have received other than Auntie Millie.

The list of witnesses called was a lengthy one, and after some further research, I found out that twenty prosecution witnesses' statements were to be tendered to the court. As one would expect, there was a lot of legal jargon that I did not understand, yet I knew instinctively that the evidence, which my mother was building in defending herself against a murder charge seemed to be working. Of course, I was not party to all that happened between them, but years later and now having access to the court papers of the case, I would dispute some of the allegations my mother made against my father! In particular, she alleged that my father physically abused her, used violence, kicked her, and constantly threatened to send her back to China or to a mental institution. She also alleged that my father would be violent to the children. None of this was true except for the China threat as my mother, in the latter part of her life, confirmed this to me. She did however say that my father's abusive language and taunts, and his manipulative way of 'twisting the words or story' would absolutely infuriate her and was as bad as physical or violent behaviour. Some of the abusive language that my father taunted my mother with was truly shocking and insulting—'you lousy prostitute, you are worse than a bargirl' and others that I did not hear. It's no wonder that my mother could not tolerate this behaviour, and with my father being the senior police prosecutor in South Kowloon Court, you could say that 'he had a way with words', which my poor mother could not possibly retaliate or challenge. To quote her words 'your father used those words against me as mental cruelty'.

I could understand her for making those allegations, and Jackson-Lipkin, in defending my mother, painted a powerful picture in the minds of the jury of a husband that mistreated his wife and was cruel and abusive to her—and it seemed to have worked! Sir Ivo Rigby in summing up the case before the jury praised the impressive defence for my mother and described the performance of Jackson-Lipkin as 'quite brilliant'.

Since I knew what I saw on the night of the stabbing, it was only a matter of time before I would be called to give evidence. I was no longer a spectator, and I would have to sit in that imposing seat next to the judge and speak in front of all those legal people and members of the jury—ugh! It was on one afternoon after the hearing session had finished, and we were just about to leave to go back to Happy Valley, that Helen Lo approached me. She seemed a kind lady, soft spoken, and yet with an authoritative presence about her. I was impressed with her thick lock of jet-black curly hair that draped over her shoulders (hairstyle fashion of the early 1970s). Helen Lo was a pioneer in the legal profession in Hong Kong, as she became the first female lawyer to have established her own practice in the colony. She became the top family lawyer, and my mother had sought help from her during the marriage breakdown. Helen Lo advanced even further to become the first female judge in the Supreme Court. I would have loved to meet her and ask her more about the case, but I only recently found out that sadly she died of cancer at a relatively young age of fifty-five in 1995. However, my one and only meeting and encounter with Helen were memorable and vivid.

'Hello Peter! I am Helen Lo. You probably know that I am here to help your mother. I am a lawyer, and your mother has seen me many times before. She may have spoken to you about her coming to see me. Can we have a little chat in a private room? I hope you and your sister are not in a hurry to leave now.'

'Oh, OK,' I said hesitantly, with my sister by my side.

As we left the main courthouse, there were long corridors leading left and right.

'Shall we go in here?'

She pushed the huge wooden door open, with a slight wooden creek sound and invited me in. She looked at me and quietly said, 'I hope your sister doesn't mind that I just talk to you alone? Then Helen turned to face my sister and said 'You must be Peter's sister?'

'Yes, she quickly responded!' My sister agreed to wait outside the corridor where there were a number of wooden chairs that reminded me of church. She seemed disappointed to be left out of the conversation.

'I promise you (my sister), it won't take long to speak with Peter. I know dinner must be waiting for you!'

With that, Helen closed the door and gestured me to sit down on a huge green leather chair that was studded on the sides and was a bit high for me to sit easily into it. It was a heavy chair! Helen pulled another chair to sit next to me and grimaced a little with the weight of it.

'I noticed that you and your sister have been coming to court to see all this happening. Are you enjoying it?' she asked with full curiosity.

I was a bit hesitant at first due to my shyness, but eventually I replied, 'Yes, it's interesting sometimes. I come here so my sister and I can still see our mother.'

Helen, with her heavy-lidded mascara eyes and rather deep red lipstick, looked straight into my eyes and nodded and her eyes blinked slowly. 'Yes, I know. It must be quite nice that you can still see your mother. She is a very brave and strong woman, you know.'

I nodded. 'I know.'

'Peter, I know it was not very nice for you to see what happened that night with your mother and father—I am so sorry for you. You are a very important person in this case for your mother, because of what you saw that night. And you are the only one who saw what happened, right?'

I nodded sheepishly.

'Peter, you have been seeing a lot of people standing in front of the judge and all those women and men giving their stories to the jury about what happened between your father and mother. What I need to tell is that the court will call you to give evidence, just like all those people you have been seeing with your sister. A nice man called Mr Jackson-Lipkin will be asking you some questions about what happened that night with your parents and especially the moment when your mother came into the bedroom looking for your father.'

Helen sighed a little, then looked very patient, and gently clasped her hands. She again looked very deeply into my eyes, awaiting a response from me. I looked down on the floor a couple of times, and I remember feeling that fear that I felt on the night of the incident. My hands were perspiring, and I could feel my body tensing. I was then feeling nervous and unsure of how to respond.

'Peter, I do understand that it could be frightening and nervous for you to stand up and speak in front of all those people. And I know that you are a shy boy but a good boy. Your father loved you very much, I can see. What you say in front of those important people in court could really help your mother. Is that what you would like?'

Once she had said 'you can really help your mother', I nodded fervently as if my nerves seemed to dissipate. I then responded enthusiastically, 'OK!'

From a rather concerned but kind expression on Helen's face, she changed to wry smile and more rapid blinking of her eyes.

'Thank you, Peter. That's wonderful. Everything will be OK. The people asking some questions will be kind and gentle. They are there to help your mother and help clear things up. You are a very brave boy, and your father and mother will be proud of you! You won't be called to speak too soon. There are still people to speak before you, so don't worry. I know you are staying with your friend Paul in Happy Valley. Are you happy there?'

'Yes, I am very happy there!'

'Good. So once I hear from Mr Jackson-Lipkin about asking you to speak, I will telephone your friend's place and let you know when it is your turn, OK?'

I nodded obediently.

Helen stood up smartly and led me to the door, with the usual creaking sound. My sister appeared suddenly and was keen to know what happened.

'Thank you for waiting for us. You are a very pretty and intelligent girl, I know. Your parents are very lucky to have such lovely children like the both of you. So off you go, and enjoy your dinner tonight. Peter, I will telephone you when I have news.'

And with that last sentence, we scampered down the corridors and headed straight for the exit. My sister in her usual precocious and inquisitive way fired off the questions.

'What did that lady say to you? Was she nice? What did you say to her?'

I was a little annoyed with her impatience and felt that she was bullying me to give her a quick answer. As we walked on to the pavement, heading towards the trams' stop, I said,

'She wants me to speak in front of all those people in court and tell them what I saw that evening between Mum and Dad.'

'And what did you say to her?' my sister retorted.

'I said OK, because it will help Mum and help the case.'

My sister understood pretty quickly that it was a serious thing I had to do, and she seemed to sympathise with me. She nodded and then said fleetingly,

'Well, if it helps Mum, it helps all of us. Don't worry, Peter. I will be with you when you speak.'

I felt relieved and assured by my sister's response for what I had agreed to do with Helen Lo. With that said and done, we travelled back to Happy Valley by tram, and we were both starving for dinner.

Paul and Auntie Millie were worried that I had returned from the court later than usual. I went straight to Auntie Millie to explain.

'The lawyer Helen Lo spoke to me after the court session. She asked me if I was willing to give evidence to what I saw that night with my mum and dad.'

'Was this Helen Lo kind and not trying to force you into doing this?' she asked with a comforting and concerned look on her.

'Yes, she was nice and friendly. She said that what I had to say in court might be very important to help my mother. So I said yes to her question.'

'Oh good! I am sure you will be OK, and that your mother will be very proud of you. You are a brave young man. God and Our Lady will be with you, Peter. We shall pray for you.'

Auntie Millie gave me a big hug, and we settled into dinner.

The phone call came from Helen Lo about a week later—I would be called to give evidence in the court at 10.00 a.m. on 21 January. Helen assured me that those asking me the questions (Jackson-Lipkin and Mr A. P. Duckett) would be gentle with their questioning and that they would understand my being a little nervous and scared of the proceedings. I was somewhat relieved to hear from Helen that my half-brother and sister would also give evidence of what they had seen on the night of the incident—meaning that I was not alone in doing this daunting task. But Helen did emphasise again to me that my evidence was the most crucial because I had actually seen the incident in the bedroom. She mentioned that the judge, Sir Ivo Rigby, may ask some additional questions, but it was only a 'maybe'. Auntie Millie and Uncle Toto were also informed by Helen that the court had invited me to give evidence, and Helen asked them if one of them could accompany me and bring me to the court hearing for that morning. Auntie Millie offered to go, and my sister would be coming along as well.

A taxi was arranged to pick us up at 8.30 a.m. from Happy Valley— enough time to have a good breakfast (my favourite cornflakes with eggs and fried spam meat) and be prepared for the most intimidating and auspicious day in my twelve-year-old existence!

It was a cool and sunny day when we arrived at the courthouse, rather different from all those previous visits my sister and I had made in the past few weeks. Auntie Mille held my hand all the way through the taxi journey and advised me to wear my best outfit—a smart tie, dark trousers, and my school blazer without a badge on it. We were early, arriving some forty-five minutes early, and were greeted by Helen at the entrance. In her usual flowing locks of jet-black hair and matching mascara and shiny knee-length boots, she smiled and looked delighted to see me, Auntie Millie, and my sister.

'Good morning, Peter! You look like such a handsome young man. Did you have a good breakfast?'

I smiled back instantly because Auntie Millie's armah had cooked a fantastic breakfast that morning.

'Yes, thank you!'

Helen turned to Auntie Millie, extended her hand out to her, and offered a greeting.

'Hello, I am Helen Lo. You must be Millie K? And hello to you (my sister).'

'Yes, pleased to meet you,' Auntie Millie replied confidently.

We walked straight to the courtroom and entered the main hall—and what a sight to see! There they were all lined-up, waiting for me this time to speak. Auntie Millie and my sister were directed to sit in the public gallery, and I was to sit next to Helen near the table where Jackson-Lipkin was to deliver his defence duties. Officials in the court were still shuffling papers in preparation for the start of the proceedings, with the jury and the judge still not in attendance. My mother had not arrived at the dock yet—I was keen to see her, and this time I was much closer from where I was sitting. Then in an orderly fashion as if by sequence, the court started to fill up, with the jury called in, then followed by Jackson Lipkin and Mr Duckett. Jackson-Lipkin moved towards me and gave me a quick smile as a way of reassuring me that everything was fine. To my left, I heard a shuffling of feet and finally saw my mother entering the court and was led to the dock accompanied by a security guard, and another gentleman to her right. Her nose was red, probably from still crying, and she was clutching a handkerchief. I managed to glance across and tried to make eye contact with her, and she gently nodded and acknowledged my presence—I was glad. Then, with a sudden movement of the court usher, the announcement was made of the entrance of the judge, and we all stood to our feet. I knew that it was my time to be called to the witness stand, and as usual my palms began to sweat and my legs felt weak. After the judge ran the formalities of the case, Jackson-Lipkin rose to his feet and announced:

'Your honour, I would like to call Peter Craggs to give evidence in the witness stand.'

Helen took my hand, smiled, and gestured me to walk over to the witness box. The creaking wooded floors didn't exactly help my nerves, and as I walked up to the stand, I had to pass by the jury box of men and women, who all looked rather serious and little sad. I was directed by one of the court ushers to stand in front of the chair. He then produced a Bible and asked me to put my right hand on it and repeat the words after him. It was the usual:

'I swear by almighty God that the evidence that I shall give will be the whole truth and nothing but the truth. So help me, God.'

I stuttered and hesitated with the words out of shear nerves and had to repeat the words and sentences a couple of times. I looked ahead at Auntie Millie who gave her supportive smile, and then to my mother who looked emotional and sad. The nearest I had ever given a statement like this was the 'Our Father' prayer we said on school assembly mornings! I managed to complete the oath with a heavy sigh. The judge to the right of me turned and looked at me with a sympathetic smile.

'You can sit down now, Peter.'

Mr Jackson-Lipkin was to cross-examine me. After stating my identity and confirming my address, he went straight into asking me as to what had happened on that late evening around 11.00 p.m.

I said I was feeling sleepy and went to bed. Then I saw my father come into the bedroom followed by my mother and the bedroom light was turned on suddenly. I described that my father stood between the beds, and my mother followed him looking very angry. I was asked by Jackson-Lipkin why my mother was angry. My reply was that my father had said something to her to make her angry. I said I heard my mother yell to my father 'You provoked me to do this.' I said I saw my mother carrying a knife and threatening him. Then I described my father trying to push the knife away as my mother was lunging at him, but my sight was obscured because my father had his back turned to me. After a struggle between them, I said I saw my father hold the left part of his stomach with his hand, and he fell to the floor. My mother left the bedroom, returned, and put the knife under the bed. I described to the court that I was so frightened that I ran out of the bedroom. I heard my mother tell my brother to call for an ambulance. Jackson-Lipkin showed me a picture of the knife used by my mother, and I acknowledged that that was the knife. I was to add one more piece of evidence, where I stated that I saw my mother drinking some brandy mixed with water at 11.00 p.m.

In all that time of giving evidence, I could see that my mother was intensely hearing what I was saying. At times, she looked at me in a strange way, a sort of distant concern that what I was saying may have a significant impact in the trial. Out of the corner of my eye, as I was retelling the events, I could see this man constantly leaning over to my mother as if they were whispering to each other. In fact, I found out later that he was an interpreter for my mother and was interpreting the English into Mandarin Chinese—my mother was always more comfortable with Mandarin, as it was her first language. Under the circumstances, I could not recall the time I had given in my side of the story, but it must have been at least half an hour.

I had more questions from Jackson-Lipkin than Duckett and was somewhat relieved because of what Helen Lo had told me before. As soon as I finished, I was instructed to leave the chair and return to the seat next to Helen Lo—what a relief! Helen smiled at me and looked pleased with what I had said. I did not look to my mother's direction or look back to where Auntie Millie and my sister were sitting—I was obeying orders!

On reflection and with more insight into what happened over the years, the evidence I had given in court did not convey the whole story of what had really happened in the bedroom. As far as I was concerned, what I had witnessed was seeing a woman who was determined to enact revenge on someone that she totally abhorred and hated, and she was determined to do some serious damage to him or indeed wanted to kill him. There was no struggle as I recall when both my parents were in the bedroom, and my mother was the aggressor. Quite vividly, I remember my father pleading with my mother, not to attack him with the knife and offering an apology to her, but she would have none of it. To me, my mother knew what she was doing and had had enough of Harry. Of course, with hindsight, if I had said this in court, would the outcome of the verdict on my mother have turned out any different . . . ?

Further questioning of other witnesses included a psychiatrist, the senior police welfare officer, a consultant that specialised in alcoholism, and three anaesthetists. In all the prevailing years, until the day I had access to the court papers, I had absolutely no idea except for the stories my mother told me about my father's drunken abusive behaviour. My father's peers had been monitoring his behaviour and there was a thorough account conducted by medical professionals, concluding that he was addicted to alcohol and had become an alcoholic and a very sick man. It was fascinating but also very sad to see that this addiction and illness was destroying his career, his marriage, and his health. The report on my mother's mental and emotional health by the psychiatrist was equally enthralling, and I could see how much of a struggle she had had with my father in trying to save the marriage and keep us children from being hurt and damaged by the whole situation.

In court, the psychiatrist's evidence stated that my father had shown all the symptoms of alcoholism namely, heavy consumption of beer, coarse digital tremor, facial flushing, frequent mood swings, irritability, unpredictability, disinhibited behaviour in the domestic situation, and abnormal sexual demands. He went on to say that in interviewing my mother, he found her an honest and cooperative witness. She had shown signs of chronic reactive depression as a result of external stress which reduces tolerance to further stress from otherwise tolerable situations. This, he said, resulted in my mother becoming unstable, leading to unpredictable and aggressive reactions. The psychiatrist went on to add that my mother was prescribed chlordiazepoxide (Librium) by her doctor to try to reduce the symptoms but said its effect was no more than palliative. The psychiatrist concluded that my mother was suffering from chronic reactive depression, which made her vulnerable to aggressive reactions due to my father's alcoholic behaviour, and with her having taken Librium and having had some alcohol herself on that night, would explain her reduced judgement and her inability to resist provocation.

When the senior police welfare officer gave evidence, I had a much clearer picture of the problems my father had in his career due to his alcoholism. In it, he said that my mother approached him in 1967 to seek help for the abusive behaviour my father was directing towards her. The welfare officer said that he had arranged to interview my father, and in that interview, he had warned him about his behaviour and drinking and that if he continued, his career in the police force would be terminated. He said that he had referred my father to a psychiatric specialist who concluded that my father was actually suffering from the alcohol addiction, which compounded to his depressed state of mind. My father had also realised that his career had virtually come to an end. He also said that my father expressed his very deep regret in having married my mother. From that interview, the officer said that he gave my father one last warning to curb his excessive drinking at which he promised the officer that he would do so. The officer said that he had also advised my mother to restrain her volatile temperament and not goad my father in regards to his poor future prospects in the force. After that meeting, the officer said, his staff started monitoring my father's behaviour, but his drinking did not diminish, so he advised the deputy assistant commissioner of administration and the assistant commissioner of police to retire my father early before he brought the force into disrepute.

Again, having to absorb this for the first time in my life, I could really see how sad and a rather pathetic figure my father had portrayed about himself probably to his colleagues and to all of us. Unfortunately, for us, the trial was further complicated by the role of the doctors in treating my father at Queen Elizabeth Hospital. In a superb preparation and defence of my mother, Jackson-Lipkin had presented compelling evidence showing that there were areas of concern in finding of medical negligence on the part of the doctors. The critical area of the failure of the doctors centred around the delay in operating on my father from the stab wound that he had received from my mother. According to Chief Justice Sir Ivo Rigby in his final summing of the case to the jury, he presented the evidence to the jury to decide whether medical negligence on the part of the doctors was a cause of death and not just the infliction of the stab wound. On 25 March, the *SCMP* 'reported on the Counsel for the defence's summing up of the case in which it stated that my mother must be acquitted of murder and manslaughter.

According to Counsel for the defence Mr Jackson-Lipkin, he argued that because of the six to seven hour delay in operating on my father, the jury could consider this as gross negligence on the part of the hospital. However, Counsel for the Crown A P Duckett for the hospital put it to the jury that the hospital doctors used their professional judgement in delaying operating on my father because of the risk to him vomiting food from his stomach. Counsel for the Crown insisted that the stab wound was still one of the causes of death and in this case it should be a case of homicide. Whatever was given in the summing of the case, it was still up to the jury to decide on my mother's fate. As far as I was concerned it seemed quite clear to me that from the reporting of the final summing-up in trial, the overwhelming evidence presented to the jury showed that the hospital had made a serious error in judgement in treating my father in the appropriate medical way. It's a small consolation; my father had lost his life. It's as if the whole system in Hong Kong had failed my father, failed my mother, as a consequence failed me and the rest of the family, and we ended up being innocent victims of an unfortunate event. When is life fair?!

On the 27th March 1972, at the trial of 'Regina v. Ng Hung alias Vicky Victoria Craggs charged with murder', was the day when my mother was to learn about her fate. Looking at the court papers, which ran to some fifty papers and typed out in the old typewriters then in the 1970s, I breathed a sigh of relief that the end of this sorry matter had arrived. My sister and I were not at the court as we were encouraged to get back to school having missed a couple of months already. I regret enormously in not attending to what turned out to be a momentous day for my mother and all us in this Craggs family. Almost precisely three months from that incident, my mother had finally arrived to a point where her freedom was about to be returned to her. My hands were shaking as I was reading the last few pages of the summing-up.

The court papers stated that the court resumed at 2.53 p.m. and described the jury of men and women as they confirmed their names to the clerk in the court. The papers then stated that the clerk asked the foreman of the jury to stand up and ask whether they had agreed on the verdict on my mother on the charge of murder. The foreman responded by saying that they had, and the clerk asked if they were unanimous, to which the foreman replied by saying that by unanimous verdict of 6 to I . . . . Then it stated that there was a sudden interruption from the chief justice who reminded the jury that the verdict of the indictment of murder must be unanimous and that they must decide whether my mother was or not guilty of murder. The foreman stated that the verdict on my mother was not guilty of murder. The clerk went to ask the foreman whether the jury had any other verdict to return, and the foreman responded by saying that they had found my mother guilty of unlawful wounding.

I must admit that I was pensive while reading through the judgement since the chief justice seemed to ask the jury to clarify their decision on the verdict.

Mr Jackson-Lipkin then appealed to the chief justice saying that in this tragic and unhappy case, that my mother could be reunited for the benefit and the welfare of the children as soon as possible. At that point, the chief justice asked my mother to stand up and stated to her that she was found guilty of unlawful wounding. He went on to say that he had no doubt that my mother bitterly regretted the stabbing and that he was satisfied it was neither in the interest of the community nor in the interest of her children that she should be sent to prison. He proposed to put my mother on a bond of $500 and commit to good behaviour for two years and stated that he was sure my mother would be able to abide by this judgement. With the agreement to the bond made by Jackson-Lipkin, he asked the chief justice if my mother could be discharged—he agreed. Sir Ivo Rigby's last parting words to the jury were that he was very grateful for their assistance, thanked them in the long and difficult case, and said he was sure that they were glad it was all over.

At 2.58 p.m., on that day, 27 March 1972, my mother was a free woman! My mother told me that the moment the jury acquitted her of murder and manslaughter but still found her guilty of unlawful wounding, she got her faith back in Jesus and God. According to Auntie Sally, who was the closest friend to my mother then and wept with joy at the decision, the sun had shone brightly as if to say 'it's the start of a new life for my mother and for her children'. The two major papers in Hong Kong: the *South China Morning Post* and *The Standard, Hong Kong, RTHK* and the local radio reported the acquittal. Luckily, for my mother, the police welfare officer was there to escort her out of the court and avoid the media scrum that was awaiting her for her comments (see copy of the front page story in the *SCMP* and *The Standard*). I had never seen the pictures or the stories reported in the press about that day until I was able to track down the archive news in the Central Hong Kong Library. Our one claim to fame in Hong Kong seemed to have drawn interest from the editors of the English language papers, covering a tragic story of a quite well-known expatriate police inspector killed by his former Chinese dance/bargirl wife—after all, it was a first in the Royal Hong Kong Police Force. Being a former journalist myself, I could see why the local expatriate community would be enticed into this classic story (a so-called 'crime of passion that would be a story of human interest') of an east-west union that went terribly wrong. What was just as painful were the comments made by some local Chinese who always concluded that a 'gweilo marrying a Chinese refugee woman' would end in disaster—east and west doesn't mix!

Speaking for myself, I was glad it was all over, and all I wanted to do and be was to be like my friends at school—normal like them. I knew my life would never be the same again, and that my relationship with my mother, my half-brother, and my sister would never be the same as before. However, it was not quite the end of the story for my father and my mother, because serious medical negligence was highlighted during the trial, and as we were to discover some ten years later, Helen Lo fought for us and won compensation from the Queen Elizabeth Hospital.

Wife accused of killing policeman

Wife denies murder

I was treated worse than a housemaid says Craggs' wife

Wife cries for joy as she is cleared of murder

VICKY Victoria Craggs broke down and wept for joy in the Supreme Court yesterday after a jury cleared her of murdering her husband, Police Inspector Charles Henry Craggs.

After deliberating for three hours, the jury of four men and three women decided she was guilty of unlawfully wounding Mr Craggs.

When Mrs Craggs was let out of the prisoner's dock, a woman friend rushed up and embraced her and both wept for joy.

Mrs Craggs was put on a $500 bond for two years by the Chief Justice, Sir Ivo Rigby.

Sir Ivo said it was neither the interest of the community nor that of the children of Mrs Craggs to send her to prison.

She has an adopted son aged 11, and a boy and a girl aged 12 and 10 respectively.

Sir Ivo said he had also considered that Mrs Craggs had been in custody for about three months – since December 20.

In evidence, Mrs Craggs admitted wounding her husband in the stomach with a knife early on December 19 at their police quarters flat at 23, Homantin Hill Road.

The stabbing followed a quarrel between the couple.

Insp. Craggs was taken to Queen Elizabeth Hospital where he died about 24 hours after being admitted.

The Crown claimed that the inspector died of the stab wound, but the defence claimed that the stab wound was not fatal.

Summing up, Sir Ivo told the jury that there should be no complete acquittal on Mrs Craggs and that she should at least be found guilty of unlawful wounding.

He told the jury that if they doubted whether the stab wound on Insp. Craggs' stomach was fatal or was a cause of death, then the Crown would have failed in the case.

He further directed that it was entirely up to the jury to decide whether there had been "gross negligence" on the part of the doctors in Queen Elizabeth Hospital.

Free, Vicky Craggs

British technicians kidnapped in Turkey

TODAY'S WEATHER

Wife cries for joy as she is cleared of murder

Preparing to Leave Hong Kong

My mother's closest friend all through the trial was Auntie Sally. Her husband, Hugh, had been very supportive towards my mother and invited my mother to stay with them in their Lai Chi Kok quarters to have some private time for reflection. It was at that time my mother told me that according to the advice of Hugh and Sally, it would be good for all us to leave Hong Kong forever, put all this behind us, and start a new life in the UK. Even with all the media attention having ceased, it was still very fresh in people's memories and that we as a family would find it almost impossible to integrate back into the Hong Kong society. This was certainly true for me at school, and I was still having a hard time in Island School. By the time of the start of the summer of 1972, my mother had made the final decision to leave Hong Kong permanently. However, there was one big obstacle before we could leave for the UK—we had no passports! Thankfully, Uncle Hugh completed all the paperwork in order to apply for British passports for all us. My mother used to say that she would always be extremely grateful to Hugh and Sally for helping us this way.

Along with getting support from Hugh and Sally, we also got support from the police welfare department, which had some legal responsibility of helping the bereaved families of former police officers. It was their job to calculate my father's pensionable service and now that my mother was a widow with three dependent children, they worked out how best we could financially be supported by my father's police service pension. My mother told me that she was somewhat relieved when the police pensions department informed her that the amount of money the family would get would be sufficient to live on. The children's allowance would support the youngest in the family until the age of eighteen years (my brother was already eighteen, I was approaching thirteen, and my sister was eleven years old). According to my mother, it was fortunate for us that they rounded up my father's service to twenty years, which was actually nineteen years and some months, and this made a big difference in the widow's pension that my mother would receive from the Government of Hong Kong.

Things were moving quickly, as my mother recalled, and she even said that she seemed to be swept by a tide of events and with not much choice in the matter. There was an organisation called the 'Anglo-Chinese Association' based in South London, and its purpose was to offer support to families that had left Hong Kong to resettle in the UK. Somehow, this organisation would offer initial settlement support to families, and the police welfare department concluded that this was the best option for the Craggs family. The association was headed by David, a Welshman, who served in the forces in Hong Kong in WWII, who had then subsequently met and married a local Hong Kong woman named Sylvia. Their connection to Hong Kong was a loose one, and they had no formal ties with the police force as such. David left Hong Kong once the war was over. He and his wife returned to the UK, a decision they bitterly regretted because they felt they had missed out on the privileged expatriate lifestyle that my parents had experienced. Since we did not know anyone in the UK (especially in South London), and we certainly did not know David and his wife, Sylvia, the police welfare service thought that this organisation would look after us—they did to a point. My mother always felt that the police authorities wanted us out of Hong Kong as soon as possible, as if they wanted to get rid of us, to wipe out everything that went on in the media, and to see us leave Hong Kong, never to return and be forgotten all out of existence. She also mentioned to me that she was concerned that we would be going to a part of the UK that we had no experience of, (except for a brief visit when were on leave) and that we would be moving to another big metropolitan city where it might be too overwhelming for us. She had also heard that London was an expensive city to live in. She had also been influenced by my father into believing that southern people, especially Londoners, were not particularly friendly. They were snobbish, prejudiced, and quite rude. I must admit from my experience of growing up there and living and working in London for over thirty years, I tended to agree with their overall judgement. Considering the circumstances and how things had been arranged for us, I suppose my mother did not have much choice or options.

My mother recalled that as a widow and with three children to look after, it was understandable that she felt extremely apprehensive about the future. In those days, there was little provision for bereavement counselling for any us, and my mother to her credit, tried to put on a brave face to rally us around and try rebuilding a family again. As far as I was concerned, I was ready to leave Hong Kong, with the only reservation that I would have to leave Paul and his parents behind. I know we were all ready to leave the trauma behind except for one person—the half-brother. He never really wanted to be a part of the Craggs unit, and he told me himself years later that given a choice, he would have remained in Hong Kong and stayed with his Chinese friends. I could understand him to a certain point, after all, he was over eighteen years old, and he had already formed his own peer group and friends that were more like family to him. The police welfare office probably strongly advised my mother that by staying together and working as a unit, we would be stronger and braver to face the challenges ahead and handle the dramatic life changes we had been through. My brother was extremely bitter about this decision, and his burning resentment and anger were all directed towards my mother. He went on to exact his revenge on her some years later in the UK! We should have left him behind in Hong Kong.

Once all the formalities were worked out, and we had our passports, the police welfare officials were arranging to get our flight tickets for London. I was still staying at Paul's, dreading the day that I would have to leave the family that I had almost adopted to be mine. My mother was still staying with Uncle Hugh and Sally and would be joined by my sister, and somehow it was arranged that they would fly to London first. My mother said the reason they flew out first was to see if she could adapt to the London environment, and see if this Anglo-Chinese Association under David's management could help us settle in. She said that if it were not suitable for all of us, she would take us back to Hong Kong and struggle through. So by June 1972, with assistance from Helen Lo sorting out all the legalities, my mother had formally confirmed to the police welfare office that she intended to leave Hong Kong permanently.

In a way I was glad I had stayed behind as long as I could, because it meant that I could have more time with Paul and Auntie Millie. I was crying a lot, expressing my unwillingness to join my mother and sister, but Auntie Millie had talked me into going to London, and she said it was important for me to give as much support and love to my mother and help her in starting a new life in the UK. With the tickets in hand for my mother and sister, we all set off for Kai Tak Airport with Auntie Millie, Paul, Kathy, and myself going along to see them off. I will never forget that day. It was a cloudy and gloomy day, the humidity was suffocating, and the weather looked like it was turning into the typhoon season. Auntie Sally had come along as my mother's most trusted friend, and she was extremely emotional. As we approached the departure gates I saw the haunted look on my mother's face, he gaunt look as if life had consumed part of life spirit, and the expression of her eyes that screamed as if to say 'where do I go from here'. The tears flowed eventually from my mother, and I tentatively approached her to give her a hug. I felt more pity for her than the feeling that I would miss her.

Auntie Millie was again her kind and compassionate self, assuring my mother that God would look after her on this new journey in her life. At that moment, I caught a glimpse of my mother's expression. I could see that she was relieved that I was staying with Paul's family. Auntie Sally was still crying incessantly, and with a turn of her head, my mother, with my sister in tow, disappeared behind the departure gates. As I was waving goodbye to a part of my family that I had become estranged from, I was thinking what a sad person my mother was and now again had to run away from a disastrous situation. I did think that if it was not because of us three children, who played a major part in acquitting her of the more serious crime of manslaughter or even the murder of my father, there was no way that she would be freed from prison so soon after having only served three months. Already fifty years old, my mother had been given another chance at life, running away almost like a refugee again, soon to be a stranger in a foreign country, with no support system and now a single parent with us on board. All that blood, sweat, and tears in running from Communist China with the dream of finding freedom, finding herself, and attracting a true loving relationship, she would've never thought that it would end in such a way. In total, my mother had only spent just over twenty years in Hong Kong, thirteen of those in the marriage to my father, and within six months since the incident, she was given her marching orders to leave Hong Kong forever. What a life, I thought, what did she do to deserve this?

I held on to Auntie Millie's hand tight, as I saw them disappear behind a line of airport security staff. I was feeling torn between needing to leave Hong Kong because of what had happened to the Craggs's and the continuing hard time I was still getting at school, and on the other hand, fighting to hang on to my identity to Hong Kong. Hong Kong was my home, it was where I grew up, where I had my best childhood, I had my best friend in Paul, and I was being protected by the love and security of Auntie Millie and Uncle Toto. I knew that it was only a matter of time when I would have to board that plane and leave my home—the thought of which gave me nightmares and tears in the remaining months ahead.

I was to find out later that my brother and I would be flying over together and join my mother and sister once they had settled down there. The timing was appropriate, with the aim for both of us to finish the summer term at school, and after the summer holidays ended, we would be ready to start the new school year in September 1972 in the UK.

We did not hear much from my mother and sister when they were staying in London. To be honest, I did not miss them at all, and all I was concerned with was appreciating every day I had left with staying with Paul's family. Auntie Millie knew how unhappy I was about leaving them, and she felt for me but still kept encouraging me to look forward to seeing my real family and expect the best for the future. As being a devoted Catholic, she often recited the rosary to the Virgin Mary, and sometimes I could hear her praying for me and for the rest of my family.

The day I dreaded the most, even more than the day I had to give evidence in court in my mother's trial, had approached. My brother had come to visit me at Auntie Millie's place, the first time that he had initiated contact with me since we were at the hospital with my father. The purpose of the visit—preparing ourselves to leave Hong Kong and face a very uncertain future in his usual abrupt manner! I remember him being rather awkward and impolite to Auntie Millie and the rest of her family, which made me both embarrassed and furious at him. It was quite obvious to Paul and the rest that we were not close, and I remember them commenting on the striking physical difference between us (I was broad and had plenty of flesh on me, while he was lean and had grown his light brown wavy hair to shoulder length). After dinner had finished and with the arrangements to meet at the airport finalised, he left in hurry and went to rejoin his friends. I felt disheartened after his visit, realising that the half-brother of mine was even more bitter and angry about going to the UK—I thought, what a prospect!

The final day had come—my last day at Paul's place—my last sight of Happy Valley Racecourse. I remember I was so churned up with emotions that Auntie Millie thought I was really ill, when in fact characteristically I was repressing my feelings. I was pretty quiet for most of the day, and Paul was trying to cheer me up. He said, 'You can watch all those English football matches live over there, have really good fish and chips, and have snow at Christmas time.'

The more he said it, the more tears started to well up in me. Paul gave me a hug and said that even with me being so far away, we would always remain the best of friends. He promised me that when he is old enough, he would come and visit me. In almost a carbon copy of seeing my mother and sister leave, we had reached the departure gates, and with only moments before we entered the area, I gazed up at Auntie Millie, who, I could see, had tears in her eyes, regretting that I was leaving their family. I don't recall saying anything to her, but I remember that she gave me the best motherly hug I have ever had. I also remember that I stared at them and that was enough of a message to them of what I was feeling at that moment. My brother called my name and gestured to me to follow him. I waved goodbye to Paul and to the rest of his family. I was approaching my thirteenth birthday, and in those few brief hours in Kai Tak Airport, I had said goodbye to a memorable upbringing and to my life in Hong Kong.

A New Life in London and the UK

There is a Cantonese Chinese idiom, which says 'Mah Say Lok Day Han', which, when translated, means: 'When the horse dies, you have to walk the path yourself'. From our former rather privileged and comfortable expatriate life in Hong Kong, we were now relegated to a very humble working-class existence when we finally arrived in London. On a cold and rather gloomy early morning arrival at Heathrow Airport, my brother was instructed to contact David at the Anglo-Chinese Association and get the address of the place where my mother and sister were now living—and where we would be living as a family. We jumped into a taxi headed towards South London. I will never forget the day when we arrived at 225A Western Road, Colliers Wood, SW19. The postcode of SW19 is more famously known for the Wimbledon Lawn Tennis Championship, but where we were headed was the poorer, industrial, and drab South London suburb of Colliers Wood.

I will never forget the day the black cab (I enjoyed the ride) dropped us outside the address. At first, I thought the taxi driver was joking with us, because the address was a fish and chip shop on a small street, and next to it was a laundrette. My brother asked the taxi driver again to make sure that that was the correct address, and he nodded to confirm that the destination was correct and pointed his finger above the fish shop—225A was written above the shop! We were both shocked, and I remember how I hesitated to take our luggage out of the taxi and walk towards the door. I looked up and suddenly saw my sister push back the curtain and wave to us—we had arrived. I think my brother was even more shocked than I was. His expression of misery added to his usual frown said it all for him. We waited a while and then heard the footsteps on some creaking floorboards. Slowly the door opened, and there was my mother and sister greeting us, wrapped up in winter clothes. The dim long corridor led us upstairs to a flat that was carpeted throughout, and for the first time in my life, I saw wallpaper throughout the flat that seemed to be ill matched to the carpet. I could see that my mother looked depressed but again tried to put a brave face on and said to the both of us, 'This is our home now. This is all we have, and we have to start all over again.' I was sad.

We could not have picked a more troubling time to start a new life in the UK. Under the Conservative government led by Edward Heath, the country was experiencing serious economic problems compounded with the industrial unrest from the coal miners, and strikes were being called by the coal unions, which was creating an energy crisis in the country. There were power blackouts, the imposition of the three-day week, and the working population seemed to be held to ransom by the unions causing maximum disruption to daily life for the UK population.

I was old enough then to understand and see that that country we had been directed to come to was going to be a very difficult and possibly impossible place for us to settle in and feel it as our new home country. After all, we had never experienced industrial strife and hearing about unions having street battles with the government, power cuts, and people not working was something akin to a living nightmare! It was clear to us that the country's infrastructure and daily life was not operating—London was not working. Sitting in our humble sitting room with candles as our only source of light, I could never have imagined that we would have to experience this in Great Britain. Not a great start or a welcome to London and the UK for the others and me, I thought!

We had our first Christmas in London as a family without my father—it was pretty miserable. I suppose it was too close to the time of when my father passed away, and it was already exactly one year ago. Despite the doom and gloom of the economic situation then, I was able to see the snowfall which delightfully blanketed the rather depressing area where we were living in. I saw other children in the street build snowmen outside their houses, and this was the first time that we tried our hand at it—one of the more pleasant things we did as a family. My mother, to her credit, tried to create a Christmas atmosphere by buying a Christmas tree from our local Woolworths, and we decorated our modest flat with the usual tinsel and lights. To lift my spirits further, Auntie Mille would write to me about once a month and encourage me to be a good boy and support my mother and the others as much as possible. She probably read about the hard economic times that the UK was experiencing, and in every letter she sent, she would include a postal order of ten pounds for my pocket money. I really missed them in those early days, and my mother could see that I was homesick for Hong Kong and Paul's family. Unfortunately, for me, this extra help from Auntie Millie drew jealous attention from my sister and brother, and this was to continue for years to come.

The flat at Western Road had a decent-sized living room and one large bedroom—for all four us! Being her pragmatic self, my mother divided the living room into two rooms effectively by putting a dividing curtain that created a small living room and bedroom. My mother and sister would sleep there, and I shared the large bedroom with my brother—it was sufficient. With our flat being above a fish and chip shop, we initially thought the smell was appetising (and we certainly had our fair share of the food), but after a couple of months, the smell became overbearing. My mother would comment that our flat smelt, no matter how hard she kept it clean. Our clothes smelt and even our hair.

We did, however, become good friends with the owners downstairs, and they sometimes would not charge us for the chips, probably because they felt sorry for us as a single-parent family. I remember the owner, George, saying that he was surprised that we had chosen to live in Colliers Wood, as the main reason why people lived there was to work near the factories. There were a number of light industry factories, which made household appliances, with one of them being the Hoover Factory. My mother knew that my father's pension did just cover our needs, but there was no spare money to pay for some small luxuries like going to London Chinatown for 'dim sum' or a proper meal. For the first time in fourteen years, since she married my father in 1958, my mother had to consider going out to work. The elder brother was approaching nineteen and was still studying in the hope to apply to university but wanted to do some part-time work to have some pocket money. I remember that my mother was so worried about finding suitable work—she had no real work skills, her English was patchy, and she felt she was too old at fifty years. That's where David and Sylvia came in to help. David's wife, Sylvia, although of Chinese ethnicity, was a typical South Londoner, having spent some twenty years in Morden, where they had a council flat. She had all the characteristics of a 'gweilo bak paw'—loud with that South London accent, gossipy, and sometimes rude. Sylvia just so happened to be working in one the factories in Colliers

Wood and suggested to my mother to apply to work on the factory floor. My mother hesitated because it reminded her of her horrible experience of working in a Chinese factory, but realising she needed to generate more income, forced herself to apply for the job.

I remember Sylvia persuading my mother, 'Don't worry, Vicky, you don't have to speak English much. The work you do is working with machines, so there is not much communication. I will be there because I am the supervisor, so if you need to speak to anyone, then speak to me.'

My mother was not that impressed, considering she didn't know Sylvia that well, and she also thought that Sylvia was a rather nosy woman. Again, being the practical person she is, my mother worked out that as a local job it would do for the time-being. It paid enough, and it would get her out of that depressing flat. With the help of Sylvia, my mother got the job—she was a presser on the assembly line that made the grills for electric fires! I was happy for my mother because she was a social person who liked to interact with people. It was a memorable day when for the first time again in my life I saw my mother get up early at 6.30 a.m. (previously, she never rose before 9.00 a.m.), nervously dressing up for her first day of work. We had breakfast together by 7.00 a.m., and then she made her way to the front door, where there was a knock on the door—it was Sylvia accompanying her to first day to the factory. From behind the curtains upstairs, we peeked out to see our mother walk together with Sylvia, both wrapped up well in the morning mist and chill, walking down the road. I kept looking as she walked in the hope that she could see me waving, and then, suddenly, she turned her head, and I saw a rather apprehensive face looking out for us, and when she did see me, she managed a gentle and innocent smile, as if it was her first day at school.

The euphoria of getting a job was soon to be wiped out for my mother. Some days she would come home in tears, complaining about her fate and what did she do to deserve this life. She said she found the work incredibly boring (as you would expect on an assembly line), all her joints hurt after pressing on some machinery, and she said that the noise of the factory would give her an earache at the end of the day. By the time she would reach home, which was about 5.00 p.m., (a shift of eight and a half hours daily), she still had to come home to prepare dinner for us—she was exhausted. Of course, I did my best in helping prepare the food, washing the rice, cutting the vegetables, always doing the washing up, but somehow she would be still upset. The noise of the factory finally took its toll on my mother, when her ears started bleeding, and Sylvia took her to see the doctor. He recommended that my mother stop work in that factory, as it could lead to her going deaf! After only having worked there for six months, my mother was out of job.

Meanwhile, I had started school at St Thomas of Canterbury Catholic School in Mitcham, a rather more upmarket area with apparently the oldest cricket club in world—The Cricketers. I did not have an easy time there, as in those days there was less of a multicultural presence in the schools in London. The way the local kids spoke in the school confused me. They spoke with their heavy South London accent and did not pronounce their 'Ts' in words like letter, water, little, bottle, and few hundred other words as well! Instead of saying hello or hi, they would greet you with 'Watcha or Hello Mate!' and the expression 'core blimey' meant something like 'awesome or wow'.

I used to be teased a lot because of my Chinese background even though I pleaded to be accepted for my English father, making fun of

Anglo-American accent, and the kids there seemed to keep their distance from me. After having spent over twenty-five years growing up in London, I am so glad that I did not pick up the accent! In 1972-73, Chinese Martial Arts had made its impact on the big screen in the UK, and Bruce Lee was the pioneer to promote it into the cinemas. I took full advantage of that to protect myself from some of the bully boys at school and to claim that 'I was really good in kung fu and not to mess with Ching Chong Chinaman Peter'. It worked!

I found it difficult to make friends with local English boys; they were either prejudiced or too yobbish to hang around with. Thankfully, I did manage to make friends that were of mixed race: Anglo-Indian, Indian, and East-African Asians (they were kicked out of Uganda by Idi Amin, and other Indians from Kenya, and Tanzania), and over the years we remained friends right up to time of sixth-form college.

My mother had recovered from the shock of losing the factory job and was determined to get another job. There were a few local hospitals in the area, looking for staff—domestic staff for some menial work. She applied and was successful. She was hired as domestic assistant at Wilson Hospital. Once again, the joy of landing a job was short-lived; it was a job of cleaning the floors and mopping the toilets. Considering that my mother had not touched a mop since her childhood days in China, she felt totally humiliated and sickened that she had sunk to this level—her pride as a 'tai tai' was destroyed. She reasoned with herself about what else could she do, and there weren't that many alternatives for her, so her drive to earn some more money kept her going in the job. My mother told me years later that the main reason she tolerated that 'shitty job' was to save some money and get out of 225A Western Road so that we all could afford to live a more comfortable life. At fifty-one years, she was still young enough to apply for a mortgage, and once she heard that, my mother was really motivated to try and apply for one. One of her few most cherished accomplishments that my mother felt proud of was that she could buy a house for the whole family by herself, especially without the help of a husband or partner! She got advice from the then Abbey National Building Society, and the only main condition was that she could maintain a steady job. She did.

Since we were short of friends, David and Sylvia visited us from time to time at Western Road, mainly due to the agreed commitment he had made to the Hong Kong Police Welfare Office that they would contact us and visit us frequently. I could see that my mother was straining to be friends with them, and the only thing that really brought them together was speaking some Cantonese and playing some mah-jong. I recall one day when they came over for tea, and my mother, like always, was cooking them a meal, she mentioned to them that she could apply for mortgage and have our own home. Once they heard that, they started discouraging my mother not to apply for one. They began making pathetic excuses saying that it 'would be too expensive and a lot of work, with having three children to look after'. I could see that they were very jealous of us and at the fact that we could afford a mortgage on a house, and this was because they had never had the opportunity or earned enough to get out of council housing that they had been living in for most of their lives. Good for my mother, I thought, and from that moment she did not mention or share anything again to that couple again and quietly and persistently by her own efforts made progress and finally was successful in her mortgage application.

My mother had found our house! In the latter part of 1973, we moved into a three-bedroomed terraced house at Whitford Gardens, in Mitcham

Fair Green. I remember so poignantly when we first walked into our new home—this time no rented flats, no government quarters, no hotels, like in Hong Kong—that really was our home! I saw my mother actually touching the four walls of the house to really feel that it was real, and she made the emotional outburst, 'I did it. After all these years, I can be proud that I have a home for my children. Even your father could not have done this!'

I did think to myself that if it wasn't for my father's pension, my mother would not have got that mortgage in the first place. She must have thought that God or my father was looking after us—it was just the boost we needed—considering the difficult economic climate in the UK at that time. For the first time I felt proud of my mother—she seemed to have her self-belief and power back in her life. I noticed also that David and Sylvia's visits to us had virtually stopped once we move to Mitcham—so much for them wanting us to be happy and successful. It was the first time that we all seemed to pull together as a family, everyone was happy—even that brother of ours!

As we settled in Mitcham for the first few years, we gradually got to know the neighbours on our street. I remember that out of a hundred terraced houses on the street, we were the only family from outside the UK. All the other residents either had been born there or had come from nearby places like Croydon, Tooting, Morden, Streatham, or Colliers Wood. Fortunately, some of the neighbours found my mother to be an attractive and charismatic person, and she made the effort to get to know them. I remember my mother telling me that a neighbour, who lived at No. 30 and was a useful handyman and had helped us fix a few things around the house, found my mother attractive and wanted to have an affair with her! My mother's response was, 'That silly, dirty old man!'

The location where we lived was almost perfect for everyone. My school was a fifteen-minute walk away, almost the same for my sister, a little more than a bus ride for my brother for him to attend a technical college in Morden, and my mother's work at Wilson Hospital was fifteen minutes bus ride away. With hindsight, I think that my mother's success in gaining a mortgage to buy a house kept us going in London and the UK. I could sense that if my mother was unsuccessful in buying the house, there was little prospect of us staying in London or UK, let alone that awful flat in Western Road. My mother confirmed to me years later that she would have arranged for us to go back to Hong Kong, if things had not worked out in London after a three-year trial experience.

My mother's confidence grew more and more, and she was proud of being a single parent. I could see that my mother was so delighted to have a large rear garden, something she had not experienced having since her childhood days in her village hometown, and certainly, there were no gardens in the time we were in Hong Kong! This is when I saw my mother showing her real background, growing up as local village girl, when she used part of the garden to grow fantastic vegetables: tomatoes, lettuce, marrow, runner beans. It was amazing to see that whatever she planted as a seed would sprout up into bulbous and great-looking vegetables. What was her secret of her having such green fingers? Answer—she used her own urine—a perfect fertiliser! As much as we appreciated having our own vegetables, which actually saved us a lot of money in food bills, it was no wonder that the garden did have a pungent smell. Luckily, the neighbours did not complain, mainly because my mother would give them a basket full of fresh vegetables. I remember my mother telling me that one of her rare fondest memories of her childhood growing up in her village was hearing the crow of the rooster at the crack of dawn making its characteristic 'Cockle doodle doo'. My mother was a country girl at heart; she liked to work on the land and see things grow, and the sheer delight that she got out of growing vegetables was one of the few instances when she enjoyed her time in the UK.

On the surface, everything was going well within the family. I noticed that my mother's relationship with my sister had become closer, mainly due to her precociousness and growing up fast—she was useful to my mother. I was the quiet one, a little slower, and my mother realised I was still affected by the loss of my father. My brother, however, was growing into a young adult, and his rebellious streak and sense of independence was causing problems. I remember on one occasion when we were cooking breakfast, in a sudden explosion of anger and rage, he threw the frying pan against the kitchen wall, with food flying everywhere and tried to smash up the kitchen. All of us were in tears, and my mother was trembling in trying to calm him down. The frustration and the resentment of coming to the UK had finally been released, and from that incident, my mother realised that she could not influence or manage that son of hers. He basically did not want to be there and blamed my mother for having ruined his childhood and the whole of his life. Fortunately, for us and for him, over the next couple of years, he was diligent enough to pass his exams, go off to study at university, and leave Mitcham.

Even years later, when he had to come back, because he failed at university (and blaming my mother again) on at least two occasions, I had to intervene to save my mother from serious injury or even death from his physical attacks on her—I should have called the police. Eventually he would move out of Mitcham again and find his own place to stay—thank

God and good riddance, I thought! More industrial disputes were to follow in 1974, and the then Prime Minister Edward Heath called an election—he lost. Although I was a young naive fifteen-year-old, I could see that the politics and the economy in the country was a mess, and there was more to come. It wasn't much better under the new Labour Government led by Harold Wilson when another economic crisis occurred in 1976 with Britain having to apply for loans from the International Monetary Fund (IMF) to keep the country afloat. It was humiliation for the UK, and the country was effectively broke. We had to endure more industrial disputes, and this time it was the refuse men refusing to collect household rubbish. Our street stank, other areas were a mess, and I vividly remember seeing mountains of rubbish piled up in Leicester Square in the heart of London—it was a national disgrace! Except for punk rock era, which was inspired by the economic chaos at the time and wanted to instigate 'Anarchy in the UK' and the disco explosion, which I found exciting, most of the 1970s was pretty grim.

All of us and like other new arrivals to the UK were getting used to the British cliché 'we muddled through' those rough times. However, something of revolution was about to take place in 1979, when for the first time in British history, the population had elected its first female prime minister, Margaret Thatcher. I recall my mother was shocked to see the news, and she commented, 'What? A woman prime minister for this country? That's ridiculous! How could a woman control a country that is so traditional? I bet you she will not last long, baloney!'

It proved to be quite an historic occasion, and the 'Thatcher era changed the face of Britain forever', so said all the commentators at that time. Meanwhile, I was getting more used to the school system in the UK and had now progressed on to secondary school, Wimbledon College. It was a catholic all-boy school, founded by the Jesuits and had instilled strict discipline in the way it handled the pupils and giving out punishment for bad behaviour—I was pretty well behaved compared to the local students! Unfortunately, for my sister, she was being bullied at school and hated it, and this led to her playing truant—she couldn't wait to leave school and start having boyfriends. My mother, on the other hand, started loathing the hospital job and wanted to quit, and she did. Now that our elder brother was out of the house, we had spare bedrooms upstairs. My mother being her pragmatic self again, and sensing an opportunity, found another way of earning an income—she could let one of the rooms upstairs to students and single people. It turned out to be quite lucrative, and my mother was relieved that she did not have to do those horrible jobs again. With spare time in her hands, she was proactive and ambitious enough to want to improve herself, especially in English so that she could have basic reading and writing skills. A Training and Opportunity Scheme (TOPS) course for older people was offered to her, and it also included basic mathematics. She was delighted to join up—and it was free!

My mother completed the course, and for her to gain a qualification was such a tremendous boost to her self-esteem. I could see that she had a direction in her life, which she had never had with my father, and she was grateful to the UK system of helping people with multiple barriers to work. With the rebellious elder brother out of the family, my mother thought that the three of us could still live happily together in this house and look forward to the future—so she thought. My sister was maturing quickly, and her interest in boys was increasing. She started rebelling against my mother and more arguments ensued between them. The close bond that they had in the last three years was evaporating fast. I know my mother was demanding at times, but I would side with her because all she wanted to do was to keep us as close as possible, considering what we had been through. For my sister, however, she had had enough and wanted to find a way to get out of the house, and by the time she had nearly reached her eighteenth birthday, she had met a boy that would take her away from Mitcham and from Mother's life for good. The young man was Simon, a typical Hong Kong Chinese, who we knew in Hong Kong when we were staying in Ho Man Tin. He had flown over to the UK to pursue his studies, but also tracked down my sister. He was the perfect vehicle for my sister to use in getting out of the house. As soon as they started dating, within a matter of weeks, my sister came home one day and said to my mother that she was leaving the family home. My mother was distraught, and she felt that she had lost the closest person to her in that time. Ever since that moment, their mother—daughter relationship was destroyed, and my mother never really forgave my sister for what she did to her. I tried my best to comfort my mother, and in some way tried to step in my sister's shoes, but it was not to be. It was like that story of the three bears 'and then there were two', and my mother and I were left in that house that had become rather empty and sad.

Despite this bitter blow, my mother continued with her training and improving her work skills. I did in some way substitute my sister when every Saturday we used to go to Tooting Market and do the weekly shopping there. I actually liked going with my mother, and what I particularly liked was buying the meat from the butchers. They were friendly, always welcoming and had a quaint sense of humour that appealed to us, and at the end of shopping with my arms aching from carrying the meat, vegetables, and fruit, we would go to our favourite cafe in the market and have a Saturday roast, delicious! The period now was the start of the Thatcher years of government, the early 1980s, and my mother was approaching her late fifties. Another TOPS course had caught her eye, this time a certificate in pattern cutting in the tailoring business. Over a period of six months, she learnt everything about the work, making jackets, trousers, and suits. I recall that my mother, as part of her project for passing the course, was to measure, cut, fit, and design a gentleman's suit to show the examiner's her skill. She had to nominate someone to design the suit for and guess who was chosen. Me! For the first time in my life, I was going to have a suit made for me and by whom better than your own mother! The suit fitted me perfectly, and I could see that my mother was proud of herself and for me. She passed the project and the course with flying colours, but for some strange reason never went to collect her certificate. It was the first time I owned a suit, and being proud of my mother's achievement, I kept the suit and wore it to a couple of my graduation ceremonies at the university.

Having completed the course, my mother was in a position to apply for work as an apprentice pattern cutter. Within a month of finishing the course, she was offered an interview for a position in a tailoring company 'Sullivan & Wooley' in the heart of the famous 'Savile Row', known for its expertise in bespoke gentlemen's tailoring. She got the job! They put my mother on a probationary period for three months where she would initially work part-time over three days a week, and if she passed her probation, she would be taken on as permanent staff and work in a full-time position. One day when she came home, I noticed a rare but familiar pleasant smile on my mother's face. I was excited about what she was about to tell me, and I sort of knew that in the envelope she passed on to me to read, there was the confirmation offer letter of employment as full-time permanent position as an assistant pattern cutter for Sullivan and Wooley Company Ltd. It was another milestone she had achieved in her working life, and it was, I believe, the proudest moment of her life, even more so, dare I say it, than being the wife of Harry Craggs!

It was approaching ten years since we first touched down at London Heathrow Airport. My mother was now nearly sixty years old, still smoking and was still reaping the harvest in the back garden. Even though we seemed to have integrated in London life as good as we can, I was still reminiscing about Hong Kong and the friends that I had left behind. The new martial arts superstar that took over from Bruce Lee was now Jackie Chan. It was an ideal way to keep in touch with some of the Hong Kong Chinese culture, and I would go up to London Chinatown to watch his new movies and any others that would give me the chance to hear Cantonese in any form of media. In 1981, out of the blue, my mother surprisingly received a letter from China—it was from her estranged daughter See Yee. I remember my mother's shocked reaction, a combination of sadness and relief that that part of her past wanted to renew contact with her. It was at least thirty years since she had heard about her daughter and from some of her cousins in China, since the country was effectively cut-off from the Western world when the Communists came to power. I remember my mother telling me that she wanted desperately to write to them and keep in touch but was advised not to because if the Communists had traced the contacts in China, those relatives would be harassed or even arrested for 'counter revolutionary' activity by being in contact with Western people. 'The Bamboo Curtain' of China was fading, and its isolation from the world was being lifted and was opening up to more Western communication and contact. My mother was excited, and she arranged to take a special holiday to visit them in China, and she would also make a nostalgic trip back to Hong Kong, almost ten years since she left there.

The trip turned out to be significant in two areas. First, it gave her the opportunity to visit Hong Kong after all the turmoil and going back on this visit gave her the chance to assess whether she could go and live there again. Although my mother had achieved so much in London in the last ten years, she told me that she still yearned to go back to Hong Kong and have a second chance of life there, but this time without my father! It was because of the children that she had forced herself to come to London, and she emphasised to me that if it were not because of that, she would have remained in Hong Kong despite the publicity she had attracted. Secondly, she did think that destiny would link her with her China roots one day, and those people she left behind would someday make contact with her, and there would be reunion again between all of them. We had been living in Mitcham for almost ten years, and in all that time, my mother had almost always rented one of the bedrooms out to a tenant, and she was able to save all this rent money over the years with the plan to return to Hong Kong some day in the near future. When she came back from the trip, I had a sense that she was quite determined to aim for this goal, but she was not sure when that would be.

At this time, I was still struggling to pass my exams to gain entry to university, and my experience of schooling in Wimbledon College was awkward and difficult. Although it was a former grammar school and had good discipline, the teachers were more focused on teaching the high achievers, while the more average students like myself were left to fend for themselves—an experience that I would rather forget than cherish! With her spirits high after the trip and after having had a 'wonderful reunion' with all her relatives,(she even went back to village in Xiaogan), my mother was ebullient and full of hope for her future, and she returned to work with a vengeance. She was now an established member of staff, having been with her employer for nearly two years, and her bosses appreciated her contribution to the company. However, about six months after that momentous trip, my mother came home in tears on a Friday afternoon. Obviously, I was concerned, and as I approached her in her usual rocking chair, she handed me an envelope—she was about to be made redundant by Sullivan and Wooley. I could see that she was both shocked and deeply disappointed and probably thought that her job was safe for at least a few more years. 'At least to work for them for five years,' she said sobbing to me. It was a cruel blow to my mother, but this development had in fact given the sign to her that her time in the UK was now limited.

She had reasoned to herself and to me that all her children had left her already, and she resigned to the fact that it was my turn that I would be leaving home to go to start university. What my mother had achieved in building a family home was now collapsing, and she could not face the prospect of living in a 'ghost house'. I was sad for her, and I did sympathise with her as she felt all alone again. After a period of self-reflection and grieving over another chapter ending in her life, my mother made the decision—she was going back to Hong Kong. With some extra money coming from her redundancy and from all the savings she had accumulated from the renting to tenants, my mother calculated that she had had enough to look after herself and to find a place to live there. She had discussed with me that I could look after Mitcham, and I could still rent some rooms out, a responsibility I found a little overwhelming, but agreed to do. My mother concluded that we had all grown up, had adopted the Western ways of independence and leaving the home, and that she was no longer needed by her children. Now she wanted her sense of independence back and having passed her sixtieth birthday, she believed she still had enough time to live a life in Hong Kong and to reconnect with her daughter and with the rest of her Chinese heritage.

The Return Years to Hong Kong

Over the period from 1983-1997, my mother spent over thirteen years in Hong Kong, and it was a big struggle for her as she recalled to me. I remember vividly my first trip back to Hong Kong in the summer of 1983, when I had the opportunity to do a project in China for my undergraduate degree. I was fortunate enough that Uncle Charlie and his wife, Mimi, would let me stay at their enormous police quarters in Cox's Road, as Uncle Charlie had known my father quite well as a colleague (Uncle Charlie had made the rank of Chief Superintendent). It was at this time that I saw my mother struggling to find accommodation, and she had to ask a favour from her old friend, Mrs Khan, to sleep on her a sofa bed at the apartment in Haiphong Mansions in Tsim Sha Tsui. Eventually my mother managed to move out and was able to rent a room in Yau Ma Tei, but once again it was a pretty awful area, and the landlady was one of the typical Chinese Taoists that would pray incessantly and burn choking incense in the flat every day. I was worried for my mother because she was well into her sixties then and should find a comfortable place to stay. She later shared with me that she was not confident about whether she could settle again in Hong Kong and that if she could afford to buy a place there.

The 1980s in Hong Kong was a time of rapid building development in property speculation, and people could buy a property as an investment, sell it out again, and make a healthy profit in six months! A friend came to rescue for my mother, Suzanna, another Chinese lady, who had married a British expatriate officer, and she gave my mother some useful advice and information into buying a flat in Sha Tin with flexible terms. Since my mother's pension came from my father's service, and it was her reliable source of income, she was successful in getting a mortgage at the age of sixty-two. In 1984, she moved into a high-rise block called Garden Rivera in Sha Tin, a pretty small but compact flat (390 sq feet), which would be her home for the rest of her time in Hong Kong. At least now, she had her own place and would not have to rely on favours from her old friends.

Over the years, I had made a number of visits to my mother in Hong Kong, mainly because I missed her, but also because I wanted to keep in touch with my former home. With contact with her daughter See Yee now established, my mother started making a few visits a year (especially over Chinese New Year) to China and started spending time with them, and by doing so, she did not feel totally isolated in Hong Kong without any family. I eventually graduated with a degree in 1985 and did not have a fixed idea about what I wanted to do with my life. I disappointed my mother because she wanted me to go back to Hong Kong and find a job there, but I was quite happy to stay in London at that time.

Due to some strange reason, I seriously considered applying for the Royal Hong Kong Police Force as they were still recruiting graduates for probationary junior inspector positions in London. I applied purely out of curiosity and managed to gain an interview. At the interview, they asked probing questions about my background and asked about my father's case and all that had happened in Hong Kong. I thought that after fourteen years since the incident, the interviewing officers would have concluded that the issue was closed and not relevant, but they still spent about half an hour on the subject. After the interview, I realised I was not interested in the position, but to my complete surprise, they offered me a position—I declined the offer. I knew in my heart that the memories of what had happened were still too fresh in my mind, and I was still too raw to face that environment again. After nearly fifteen years of my mother's acquittal from the Supreme Court, Helen Lo contacted my mother to give her some good news. Helen had been fighting for compensation for us for the alleged medical negligence of the doctors at Queen Elizabeth Hospital when they had treated my father there. My mother was awarded damages by the hospital, and we would all get a share of the money for the trauma that we had suffered. In addition to this, the British government informed my mother that she would also be entitled to another pension in addition to the widow's pension, which she was receiving from my father's service to Hong Kong Police Force. My father's status was termed as 'Her Majesty's Overseas Civil Servant', and all his years of service in Hong Kong meant that my mother would be entitled to the widow's overseas pension allowance from the then Crown Agents.

My mother put the money to good use, and she was able to pay off the remainder of the mortgage she had on her flat in Sha Tin. This extra money also meant that she was also able to fly back to the UK more often and spend time with us—something she cherished over the years. It also meant that she had more disposable income, and this, I am afraid to say, made me dependent on her for money when I was hard up. I resented my mother receiving so much more money at the expense of my father's death, and I used this against my mother to make her feel guilty about what she had done. She acquiesced, and, over the years, helped me with thousands of pounds to the rage and envy of the other two members of the family. To her credit, my mother tried to be fair to all of us, and she did her best to help the others and me financially whenever we needed that support.

Even though my father had left me for more than fifteen years, in death, he was still looking after me through my mother and, indeed, was helping the other two as well. This situation caused a lot of stress for my mother, and she would often curse my father that his 'death money' caused her more misery than happiness. She seemed to think that she was entitled to all the money as well because she argued that this was a payback for all those years that she had suffered in being married to my father. Unfortunately, this sorry state of affairs was always a burning issue that divided me and damaged my relationship to my mother right up to her death. My argument to her was that we were all victims of this tragedy, and there were no winners in this. Alas, she did not agree to my conclusion.

Time was moving on for my mother and as much as she enjoyed her independence in Hong Kong, inevitably the ageing process took its toll on her when she discovered that she was diabetic. She was still smoking right up to her seventieth year. Realising her health was failing as she was aging, she began to miss us more in the UK. Hong Kong was fast approaching its return to sovereignty to the motherland China, and in my view, the local media had stirred up a mild panic, reporting that the reversion to Chinese rule would be a disaster for Hong Kong, its prosperity, and its freedom. The media succeeded to a certain level as thousands of middle-class Chinese applied for emigration mostly to Canada in the belief that they would have a better future for themselves and their children. I recall watching the handover ceremony in London's Dockland's where the first Chinese immigrants had settled in London and where the first Chinatown had started. It was a highly emotional occasion for me and for the hundreds of others who were watching it live on a big screen. It was the end of an era as the Hong Kong I had known up until then was under British rule. To see Chris Patten, the last governor of Hong Kong, with his head bowed as if in mourning—signified the end of the empire. Even before the handover ceremony started, the omens were not good when we heard in the news that a freak accident had occurred during the street celebrations when a flotilla crashed into the waiting crowds lining the streets in Hong Kong killing two British tourists. Added to this was the weather on the day. It couldn't have been more atrocious when on the eve of midnight of 31 July, leading into the 1st of July 1997, it was absolutely pouring down with rain in Hong Kong. I saw Prince Charles, who was representing the Queen, wearing what looked like a plastic overall covering over his white colonial uniform, protecting him from being totally drenched in the rain. I thought it was a rather pathetic sight of a prince covered in plastic, and it conveyed to me a very sad day and an ungallant image of a former great British Empire in the East. My mother, however, gave the impression that she was worried that Hong Kong would be chaotic, when, I believe, in fact, that she had had enough of the place and wanted to have the last remaining years of her life with her children in the UK. Just after the handover, I flew back to Hong Kong to help my mother complete the sale of her Sha Tin flat, which, luckily for her, made a healthy profit, and it was to be the end of her experience of living in Hong Kong for the rest of her life. There was the question of where she would stay when she returned to London, and it was arranged with my brother that my mother could stay upstairs in Mitcham. I think my mother wanted to see if she could patch things up with him, and for a while, they managed to tolerate each other. However, the reconciliation was short-lived, and my mother had to think about her next move.

The supposed chaos and ruin that China might have caused since its takeover never really materialised, when, in fact, Hong Kong continued on in its merry way of making money and maintained its status as a major financial and technology hub of East Asia. For all those Chinese that emigrated to Canada and having secured their passports after a number of years realised that they may have made a mistake in leaving Hong Kong in such a panic. Some of them told me that emigrating and living there felt like 'they had served a prison sentence', and were not particularly happy about their decision to move there. Besides, Hong Kongers knew that they would never earn as much money in their new residence, and they were hurting. Within a few years of Chinese sovereignty, they could see that not that much had changed since the handover, and the Hong Kong they had left was still prospering. A lot of them went back.

Nearing the End

The last decade of my mother's life was mainly spent on the mainland and having to rely on her daughter See Yee and the in-laws. She made the decision to go back to China having had a rough time with my brother in Mitcham, which lasted for about two years from 1997-1999. Mitcham was now divided into two flats, with him buying downstairs from my mother, and she still owned the top flat. The relatives in China promised that they could look after her, since See Yee was now retired from working as a doctor in the hospital. They were now living in Guangzhou, and this attracted my mother because she thought this would be convenient enough for her to make the occasional visit to Hong Kong. I had accompanied my mother back to Hong Kong and Guangzhou to support her and to see if what See Yee had offered was sincere and genuine. After all, she had abandoned this daughter of hers for most of her life, and they had not really spent much time with each other. My mother also had her reservations about them because she sensed that they had changed from their humble upbringing when they were living in the countryside—she was right. China had now become more materialistic, and the people had become greedy and corrupt—and See Yee and her family had followed suit to a certain extent because now they had become city people with the move to China's third city Guangzhou. All I wanted for my mother was that she could have a home for the last part of her life and be with people she could trust. Things seemed to have gone well between them, and to my surprise, my mother offered to buy an apartment for them with cash so that they would be close to each other. Their apartments were in fact next door to each other! My mother asked me a few times whether she was doing the right thing, and I responded by saying that as long she was happy about doing it, I would support her. In my limited Mandarin, I asked See Yee if she could look after our mother, and her reply was 'I will do my duty and try my best'. With that answer, I relayed this back to my mother, who seemed to accept this as one final confirmation she needed to hear and gave her the confidence and the go-ahead to buy the two apartments together. However, there was always a hint of doubt whether they could fulfil their duty to my mother, and I did warn her not to expect too much from this daughter—she knew what I meant.

There was to be one more happy reunion for all us in early 2000 and one that when I look back I was extremely proud of. My sister had now become a mother and had a four-year-old daughter, and she was a delightful young girl. I had now been married for three years to a Chinese woman, who I met in London, and who coincidentally came from Guangzhou. My mother wanted all of us to come over and spend a Chinese New Year together, which also included my brother. It was the one and only time that as three siblings we would be able to travel together to China and visit my mother—a trip that I had arranged from start to finish and one that turned out quite well. For the first time, the Chinese relatives would meet all of us together, including my sister's daughter and my then wife. Since I had only a registry marriage in London, my wife and I decided that since everyone was in Guangzhou, we should hastily arrange a Chinese wedding ceremony to fulfil the Chinese side of the union. We managed to book the celebration at the well-known White Swan Hotel, and the occasion was an overall success. I could see that everyone was happy for us. It was the last union between all of us, the British and the Chinese sides, something that I knew would not be repeated again.

The honeymoon period of my mother's coexistence with her daughter See Yee and the rest of the in-laws was now showing big cracks of tension and arguments between them, ever since my mother decided to live with them in 1999. According to my mother, she could not tolerate their greed of more money and incessant demands for a more material life, and they had formed the impression that my mother was a wealthy overseas widow who had lots of investments stashed away in foreign banks. My mother's constant phrase to describe them as a 'deep black hole that could never be filled' was perceptive and accurate, and I saw what she meant in the times I had visited them in Guangzhou. My mother naively thought that buying a flat for cash for See Yee would make her and her husband treat her better, when, in fact, it turned out to be the opposite. They became even more demanding of my mother to give more money (paying for the maid to cook, clean, buying expensive furniture), and this friction and tension between them eventually destroyed the relationship. Once See Yee had her name on the flat, within the year since owning it, she was making plans to move out with her husband and buy a place away from my poor mother. The warning that I gave my mother, alas, turned out to be true, and I do believe that my mother probably knew that as well but was in denial of the evidence. Besides, my mother told me later that the mother/daughter relationship could never have been patched up as there was too much distance between them, and my mother probably insulted See Yee by describing her father as nothing but a 'playboy and a useless husband'. I was not around to see what was going on between them (thank God), as I only heard the story from one side, my mother. She was in her eighties now, and I know she was getting more difficult and miserable with age and showing signs of going senile, and because of that See Yee and the others found it difficult to cope with her. It was the last blow that my mother could cope with from her supposed nearest and dearest.

Bruised, hurt, and deeply disappointed with these people, my mother, as she had all through her life, picked herself up one more time and battled to survive on her own without them. I tried to give more support to my mother, and I would fly over and visit her to see that she was all right, and even my brother would spend some time with her in China. My brother, to his credit, did give my mother some good advice in one last help when he suggested she could buy herself a place called Clifford Estates in Panyu. It is a massive private development of apartments, which must have a population of at least one hundred thousand residents and is only an hour's bus ride to the centre of Guangzhou and a two and half hours coach direct to Hong Kong and to the international airport. Apparently, more than fifty per cent of the residents living at Clifford are from Hong Kong, who bought an apartment there as a holiday home as it was relatively cheap by Hong Kong standards. My mother bought a comfortable two-bedroomed apartment there in 2004—enough distance from those estranged relatives, but close enough that they would come by once a month and take her out for lunch.

My mother now had alienated herself from both sides of the family, something that she tried hard to avoid but seemed to always sabotage her own intentions. Meanwhile, my life in London had taken some significant downturns when my marriage failed, and we were living separate lives. My work prospects were limited, and I was looking for something different to do. My mother's health was clearly deteriorating and she being on her own again with only the Chinese servant, as her companion, I felt I needed to support her. I offered to go to China and Hong Kong and spend that time with her and also try my luck there. My mother was glad to hear that I was coming, and I remember her words saying 'come and spend the last few years of my life with me', as if she knew that was all the time she had left—she was right. The two years I spent with my mother were divided between Hong Kong and at Clifford Estates, and I used to commute back and forth for work, which I found exhausting at times. My mother even did some renovations to the apartment to combine two small rooms into one large bedroom for me to make my stay as comfortable as possible, and this I greatly appreciated. This time staying with her, I got to know a side of my mother that I had not seen before. I had seen my mother returning to her Chinese roots, almost always speaking Mandarin with me, adopting a very economical lifestyle, almost like the time of childhood days and watching a lot of Chinese television (CCTV) on drama and the old history of the country. The only thing British she maintained at Clifford was her favourite three to four cups of English tea each day and having some proper chips at one of the Western restaurants at the estate or in Guangzhou. Although it was pretty cheap living in Clifford, my mother always seemed to have problems hiring good domestic maids. She needed them to not only clean and cook for her, but also to offer some companionship and share some time together. Her expectations again were too high as these servants had little or no education and had very heavy local accents that my mother could hardly understand, since most of them had migrated from their villages of south-western and western China to look for better paid work in the city. In the two years that I was there, she must have hired and fired at least six servants! One day I sat my mother down to have a good heart-to-heart—living like this was not the answer. I could see she was struggling to hang on to her independence, the servants were not capable of looking after her, the Chinese relatives were distant, the heat in the summer at Clifford was dangerously hot (hitting 40°C in the summer), and her health was deteriorating fast. Besides, my work in Hong Kong and China was on contract, and it would not last beyond two years. I had to point out to my mother that she had two options—either come back to the UK or consider moving back to Hong Kong. She opted to try Hong Kong again because she thought that a couple she had made friends with at Clifford would be able to look after her in their apartment in Sha Tin (again!). I remember the day that we packed to go to Hong Kong, I saw my mother using sheets to cover the furniture at Clifford, and I wondered whether she would ever return to this place—it turned out that she would never see it again. I promised my mother that I would do my best to look after the place, and with some tears in her eyes, she nodded and walked out the front door. As our coach was waiting for departure to Hong Kong, my mother took a deep sigh, looked out the window for the last time at the Clifford Resort Centre, and waved goodbye to her life there and to her life in China.

The arrangement she had with her friends, Mr and Mrs Wong, turned out to be a failure. She tried staying with them in their modest flat in Sha Tin but found out that it was totally unsuitable and ended up staying in the Regal Riverside Hotel in ShaTin. She was now in a confused and anxious state; the Hong Kong idea did not work out, and she was not that keen in coming back to the UK with me. The summer of 2007 turned out to be an extremely hot one, and I could sense that my mother was disillusioned and depressed about her situation. She even floated the idea of buying a flat in Hong Kong again, but I knew that she did not want to live that solitary existence again. One late afternoon I got a phone call from the hotel—my mother had suffered a heart attack. I knew it was serious because I was advised to go the Prince of Wales Hospital immediately, with my mind saying to me 'get her back to the UK if she survives this'. She managed to pull through by a minor miracle, but the warning signs were there—it was time to take her back to the UK and let her spend her remaining days with me and my sister. She needed to have an angioplasty, which went well, and she having made a recovery, I decided for her that we would fly her back to the UK. Yet I knew that my mother's days were numbered, and she had lost a lot of weight. Her usual fight for life was considerably diminished and now she was wheelchair bound. This time it really was a goodbye to Hong Kong and China. She was off to spend her last days with the British side of her children.

Unfortunately, the last of year of my mother's life was to cause her more pain for herself and for the rest of us. In her years spent in China, she had somehow contracted tuberculosis, which appeared as a lump on her neck, and I was advised to take her to see a specialist. A date on Christmas Eve was arranged for her to have the lump removed, and after the operation she had to stay overnight at the hospital. My mother attempted to go to the toilet by herself, fell heavily, and broke her hip—in the early hours of Christmas morning! Her one-night stay became a four-month recuperation and rehabilitation bedridden stay in that awful hospital. She still had some fighting spirit left in her. She recovered and surprised the nurses in the hospital that she was still able to walk with Zimmer frame, but now we had to put her in the nursing home. Incredibly, the biopsy as well as the blood test results for my mother's condition were missed and never recorded by the hospital, and there was no confirmation that the lump removed was TB. This turned out to be disaster for my mother when some months later when I visited her in the home, she looked painfully thin and weak—the TB had returned! It was extremely fortunate that my mother didn't pass on the TB to other residents in the home as it is highly contagious. She was given drugs for the treatment of TB and had to be isolated from the rest of the residents—very depressing for my mother, because it kept her away from some of the friends she had made in the home. My mother reacted terribly to the drugs and was immediately rushed to the accident and emergency with 80 per cent skin loss in her body. Her condition was a rare reaction to TB drugs treatment called Toxic Epidermal Necrolysis (TEN), and this time she was dying. I thought that I had seen enough traumas in my lifetime already, but this time I saw my mother disintegrating in front of me, and she could not fight this one any more. I was heartbroken and so were the others, and there was nothing the doctors could do to save her. After seven tearful and painful days, my mother lost her life at the age of eighty-six, on 2 December 2008.

I am one to believe in coincidence, and this time it was my mother's turn to have experienced and become a victim of hospital incompetence and negligence. Since my mother's death, an inquest into her death followed six months later, and the coroner found that there were substantial areas of what he called 'systemic areas of failure' in the management of my mother's care in the NHS hospital. I followed up on this, made an official complaint to the chief executive of the hospital, who in turn issued me an official apology to the failures of the hospital concerned. Now it was a matter of compensation, and as cruel, as that may sound, legal regulations and the compensation culture of the NHS Trust meant that discussions focused on working out how severe this negligence was worth in financial terms and coming to an appropriate financial settlement that would be acceptable to the NHS Trust and us. It seems this was the only and last gesture to have complete closure on this tragic matter. Now as a mature adult, I had managed to contain my rage and frustration at such incompetence and also the fact that history had repeated itself in seeing this could happen to my last and only parent. The cliché 'life isn't fair' accurately sums up for me what I and the other two in the family have had to experience in this lifetime. As I write, the three siblings left in this family are in the final stages of getting compensation from the authorities and put an end to this sorry chapter. One thing is certain for me from this experience, in that I will make sure that when it's time for me to leave this planet, I will make damn sure that I will *not* let myself be a victim of government hospital incompetence!

I believe that my mother really did live a life of 'blood, sweat, and tears!' From all the stories she told about her life (and I am sure there was a lot more that she did not want to divulge to me), it was an extraordinary life in so many aspects. Going by the Chinese calendar, my mother was born in the year of the dog—*gau*. It's pronunciation is almost similar to the number nine—gau. She once said on reflection on her life that she had nine lives. She survived the unhappiness in childhood, the disaster of her first marriage, the Japanese invasion, she survived the Communist revolution, she survived the vice world in Shanghai, and in Hong Kong, and survived the marriage to Harry, survived her prison experience, and survived the trial of the death of my father. She even survived the first heart attack in Hong Kong in 2007—she truly lived up to her Chinese animal sign!

In the final few years of her life, I did ask my mother again whether she regretted the stabbing of my father, to which her answers were inconsistent and contradictory. I knew that she could not tolerate the life she had been living with my father and that something *big* had to happen between them to sever their relationship. She used to say 'all because of that lousy $500 that your father gave me that night'. Yet, uncovering more about their relationship in their final years together I was to come across some information that I had never known about or at least did not realise that another significant issue that provoked my mother to take drastic action and put an end to this unhappy marriage. In the last few years of my mother's life, she revealed something to her one and only friend—Lily. Lily told me that the other main reason she stabbed my father was because he wanted to return to the UK and be with the real love of his life, Cousin Audrey. He would divorce her in Hong Kong and return to the north-east with me and perhaps my sister. My mother would be left with the illegitimate son of hers, and they would both be left on their own to fend for themselves. I could imagine the rage and resentment my mother must've felt towards my father, and the horror she must've felt at being abandoned like that. After all, my mother then was approaching fifty years, and with a troubled son by her side, her prospects must have looked extremely depressing. The ghost of desperation and anxiety had visited my mother again—like so much of her life!

Yet on the other hand, she would contradict herself when I asked her whether she had any regrets marrying a Westerner. As we were waiting in the lounge to fly back to the UK for the last time, I could see that my mother was in a sombre and reflective mood.

'Mum, if you could live your life all over again, would you have still picked a gweilo to marry?'

She gazed ahead for a moment, looked down, then suddenly straightened her back, and said adamantly, 'Yes, absolutely!'

As a true survivor and battler of life's obstacles, my mother still had the maternal instinct of keep this family together in the best way she knew how, but with so many scars from the Hong Kong experience, her hold was a tentative one. As we had all grown up in the UK and learnt about the so-called 'individual freedom and having the choice to live our lives as we see fit', this attitude actually caused more division and tension between all of us than giving us liberation. When my father died so suddenly, that incident brought us together to face the struggles of making a new life in a foreign country and sometimes dealing with a hostile environment. With my mother's passing, the final crack in the not-so-strong bond of the family tore us apart and dealt the final blow to end our association with each other. It was further proof that the mother figure is pivotal in holding a unit together.

As close as I was to my father in the final few years of his life, my relationship to my mother in the latter part of her life was just as intimate. The crucial difference between the two was that I had an adult relationship with my mother, and growing up with her over the years gave me the opportunity to understand the personality that was my mother. Although she had taken my father's life, the one person that I truly loved, over a period of time, I was able to forgive her. It became clearer to me that for me to move on (and to come to terms with the loss and bereavement) with my life, it was crucial for me to make 'my peace' with my mother and have as little resentment or bitterness towards her before she left this world. I certainly did not want to be in the position of my half-brother! The sad thing for my mother, however, was that she never really forgave herself for not being, to quote her own words to me, a 'better wife, a more loving mother, and a kinder person'.

There is no doubt in my heart and mind that my parents were fated to meet each other and that it was a kind of 'fatal attraction' that had brought them together. They became lovers and eventually husband and wife. For all their trials and tribulations, their strengths and weaknesses, addictions, drama, in a perverse way, I wanted these two individuals to be my parents in this lifetime. Whether I have inherited some of their characteristics—and indeed it's probably natural that I have most of their traits—my own path in the world has been one of great challenges, dramas, and moments of exciting adventures. Such characters like my father and mother seemed to represent a time that really was from another world, a period in history that had the extremes of human existence and the struggle to keep their heads above water. Yet even nearly forty years since my father left me (and three years since my mother has passed away), I feel their presence in my life. They say time is a great healer, and indeed, it is, and since I had decided to write this memoir to them, the tragic events still remain fresh in my mind after all these years. It's as if that examining and deciphering all the court papers, reading through all the newspaper stories, and of course seeing the pictures of my parents seemed to have resurrected them. From all the trauma that I had suffered and witnessed (not forgetting my half-brother and sister, who suffered in their own way), and the depths of despair and disillusionment I had sunk into, my decision to dig up all the unpleasant past and having to recount all that unpleasant history of events was, in fact, as it turned out, the best possible therapy for me. It was better than all those hours of counselling and therapy I had over the last twenty years! I have come full circle having returned to Hong Kong. Completing this research has given me a sense of completion and closure. I am proud to have had these two individuals in my life, and they gave me a childhood experience that only a few had in those times in the world. They, of course, made me the person I am today. With that, I could only come to one final realisation: Harry and Vicky Craggs were my parents, and I loved them dearly, and I still do to this very day!